# A Christmas Miscellany

IAN JACKMAN

EDITOR

# A Christmas Miscellany

Random House Reference
New York • Toronto • London • Sydney • Auckland

Copyright © 2005 by Ian Jackman

Please address inquiries about electronic licensing of reference products for use on a network, in software or on CD-ROM to the Subsidiary Rights Department, Random House Reference, fax 212-572-6003.

This book is available for special discounts for bulk purchases for sales promotions or premiums. Special editions, including personalized covers, excerpts of existing books, and corporate imprints, can be created in large quantities for special needs. For more information, write to Random House, Inc., Special Markets/Premium Sales, 1745 Broadway, MD 6-2, New York, NY, 10019 or e-mail specialmarkets@randomhouse.com

Visit the Random House Web site: www.randomhouse.com

Interior design by Elina D. Nudelman

Library of Congress Cataloging-in-Publication Data

A Christmas miscellany / Ian Jackman, editor.
p. cm.
Includes index.
ISBN 0-375-42604-3
1. Christmas—Miscellanea.   I. Jackman, Ian.

GT4985.C542  2005
394.2663—dc22        2005049411

First Edition

0 9 8 7 6 5 4 3 2 1

# Contents

# Introduction

What do we think of when we think of Christmas? Wide-eyed children write letters to Santa Claus promising to be good. Then, the night before Christmas the kids try to stay awake to see Santa deliver his bounty, curious as to how he gets in if the house has no chimney. For weeks, the stores are stuffed with Christmas cards and decorations; baubles and trinkets; holiday food and drink. Shoppers shop steadily, and then throng to the markets hunting for last-minute bargains. Families and friends pick up gifts for their families and friends. Families get together to eat and drink and exchange presents on Christmas Day in houses trimmed for the occasion, a brightly-lit tree as the centerpiece. Some people go to church to celebrate the birth of Christ, and it's a time when the fortunate show charity for those less fortunate. By the end of the nineteenth century, these familiar elements of a modern Christmas were solidly in place.

Newspapers and magazines of the time were full of seasonal stories and light verse and practical advice for the holiday. You could find recipes (or "receipts," as they were often called) for the dinner staples of roasted turkey and English plum pudding, together with full menus for breakfast, luncheon, tea and dinner. You could also find out how to decorate the tree and get the house ready for guests. There were annual reminders of gift-buying etiquette and suggestions for parlor games to fill up the time between one meal and the next.

This *Miscellany* includes pieces from newspapers, magazines and books published from the 1880s to 1917 to give a flavor of how this old-fashioned Christmas was celebrated. We begin with three short stories and a selection of verse that illustrate the sentiment of the holiday in the popular media. There are newspaper accounts of Christmas in the White House and at the front lines in France in 1917 along with selections of menus and recipes, prices of food in markets in Washington, D.C., in 1915 and a story about shopping for a cheap turkey in Washington Market, New York, in 1898.

Alongside the instructions for decorating the tree and buying cigars as presents, there were frequent pieces in newspapers and magazines lamenting how much Christmas had changed. It's clear that bouts of seasonal nostalgia have been hitting men and women of a certain age for at least a hundred years, because even a century ago, Christmas just wasn't what it used to be.

There can be few of us who haven't listened politely as an older relative reminisced about the holidays of their youth. Here, we read the same sentiments, coming from people like the gentleman the *Brooklyn Daily Eagle* (a newspaper Walt Whitman edited in the 1840s) called a "Christmas Croaker": "The season starts too early; it's too commercial; there's too much pressure to buy and indulge. And the weather's no good for sledding these days either."

Part of the period from which these stories are taken is the "Victorian" age, in Great Britain at least. If the grousing about the commercialization of Christmas is ageless, the Victorian preoccupation with the fate of the lower classes has dated more readily. Jacob Riis, bestselling author of *How the Other Half Lives* (1890) and champion of the rights of tenement dwellers, provides two pieces in the *Miscellany*. In the first, he looks at Christmas among the poor of New York. Riis goes to church, and writes,

> It is easy to pick out the children in their seats by nationality, and as easy to read the story of poverty and suffering that stands written in more than one mother's haggard face, now beaming with pleasure at the little ones' glee.

Again and again, in story after story of the time, Christmas briefly lifts the agony of unmitigated hardship, or it doesn't, as orphans and invalids die lonely deaths far from their families. A good family will solve every problem, as the narrator of our first story, "An Old-Fashioned Christmas," finds. Now an older man of perhaps forty, Mr. Christopher is looking for the elusive "Old-Fashioned Christmas." He isn't specific as to what he's looking for, but he finds it amongst children. The selections in the *Miscellany* show us, if we needed to be shown, that these holidays are for the kids; for children writing to Santa Claus, whose requests are opened at the Dead Letter Office in Washington, for the little boy eating Christmas dinner with his grandfather, and for our Christmas versifier wondering what it will be like when Santa Claus is President.

The second piece by Jacob Riis asks: "Is There a Santa Claus?" It is sentimental but uncynical, and an antidote to the gripes of the Christmas Croaker. Riis's interviewer has him, and us, figured out. When we think about an old-fashioned holiday, we're thinking of our own childhood, when we believed in things like Santa Claus. In the delightfully archaic prose of the time, our correspondent notes,

When a man has passed middle life his capacity of enjoyment decreases rapidly, and it is not remarkable that he should retain a fondness for the ways and customs of his youth, when keen delight was possible, and the canker worm of disappointment had not appeared upon the scene.

In the spirit of all our pre–canker worm times, we offer this selection.

# Stories

# "An Old-Fashioned Christmas"

FROM *THE SATURDAY EVENING POST*, DECEMBER 9, 1899

Richard March

"An old-fashioned Christmas—a lively family will accept a gentleman as paying guest to join them in spending an old-fashioned Christmas in the heart of the country."

That was the advertisement. It had its points. I was not sure what in this case an old-fashioned Christmas might happen to mean. I imagined there were several kinds of "old-fashioned" Christmases; but it could hardly be worse than a chop in my chambers or—horror of horrors!—at the club, or my cousin Lucy's notion of what she calls the "festive season." Festive? Yes! She and her husband, who suffers from melancholia, and all the other complaints which flesh is heir to, and I, dragging through what I call a patent-medicine dinner, and talking of everybody who is dead and gone, or else going, and of nothing else.

So I wrote to the advertiser. The reply was written in a sprawling, feminine hand. It was a little vague. It appeared that the terms would be five guineas; but there was no mention of the length of time that fee would cover. I might arrive, it seemed, on Christmas Eve, but there was no hint as to when I was to go, if ever. The whole thing was a trifle odd. There was nothing said about the kind of establishment which was maintained or the table which was kept. No references were offered or asked for. It was merely stated that "we're a very lively family, and if you're lively yourself you'll get on uncommonly well." The letter was signed "Madge Wilson."

Now it is a remarkable thing that I have always had an extraordinary predilection for the name Madge. I do not know why. I have never known a Madge. And yet, from my boyhood upward I have desired to meet one. Here was an opportunity offered. She was apparently the careworn mother of a "lively family." Under such circumstances she was hardly expected to be "lively" herself; but her name was Madge, and it was the accident of her Christian name that decided me to go.

I had no illusions. No doubt the five guineas were badly wanted; even a "lively family" would be hardly likely to advertise for a perfect stranger to spend Christmas with them if they were not. I did not expect a princely entertainment. Still I felt that it could hardly be worse than a chop or cousin Lucy; the subjects of her conversation I never cared about when they were alive, and I certainly do not want to talk about them now they are dead. As for the "pills" and "drops" with which her husband doses himself between the courses, it makes me ill even to think of them.

On Christmas Eve the weather was abominable. All night it had been blowing and raining. In the morning, it began to freeze. By the time the streets were like skating rinks it commenced to snow. And it kept on snowing; indeed, it turned out to be, quote, a record in the way of snowstorms; hardly the sort of weather to start for an unknown destination "in the heart of the country." But at the last moment I did not like to back out. I said I would go, and I meant to go.

I had been idiot enough to load myself with a lot of Christmas presents without the faintest notion why. I had not given a Christmas present for years—there had been no one to give them to. Lucy cannot bear such trifling, and her husband's only notion of a present at any time was a gallon of somebody's Stomach Stirrer. I am no dealer in poisons. I knew nothing of the people I was going to. The youngest member of the family might be twenty, or the oldest ten. No doubt the things I had bought would be laughed at; probably I should never venture to offer them. Still, if you have not tried your hand at that kind of thing for ever so long, the mere act of purchasing is a pleasure.

I had never enjoyed "shopping" so much since I was a boy. I felt quite lively myself as I mingled with the Christmas crowd, looking for things which might not turn out to be absolutely preposterous. I even bought something for Madge—I mean Mrs. Wilson. Of course I knew that I had no right to do anything of the kind, and was aware that the chances were a hundred to one against my ever presuming to hint at its existence.

I was actually ass enough to buy something for her husband: a box of cigars. What the "lively family" would think of a perfect stranger arriving burdened with rubbish, as if he had known them all their lives, I did not dare to think. No doubt they would set him down as a lunatic.

It was a horrible journey. The train jolted along in a laborious fashion at the rate of about six miles an hour, stopping at every roadside hovel. I counted seven in a distance, I am convinced, of less than twenty miles. When at last I reached Crofton, my journey's end, it turned out that the station staff consisted of a half-witted individual who was stationmaster, porter and clerk combined, and a hulking lad who did whatever else there was to do. No one had come to meet me; the village was "about half a mile," and Hangar Dene, the house for which my steps were bent, "about four miles by the road": how far it was across fields my informant did not mention.

There was a trap at the Boy and Blunderbuss, but that required fetching. Finally, the hulking lad was dispatched. It took him some time, considering the distance was only "about half a mile." When the trap did appear it looked to me uncommonly like an open spring cart. In it I was deposited with my luggage. The snow was still descending in whirling clouds. Never shall I forget the drive in that miserable cart, through the storm and those pitch-black country lanes. We had been jogging along some time before the driver opened his mouth.

"Be you going to stop with the Wilsons?"

"I am."

"Ah!"

There was something in the tone of his "Ah!" which whetted my curiosity, near the end of my tether though I was.

"Why do you ask?"

"It be about time as some one were to stay with them as were a bit capable like."

I did not know what he meant. I did not ask. I was beyond it. I was chilled to the bone, wet, tired, hungry. I had long been wishing that an old-fashioned Christmas had been completely extinct before I had thought of adventuring in quest of one.

We passed through a gate, which I had to get down to open, along some sort of avenue. Suddenly the cart pulled up.

"Here we be."

That might be so—it was a pity he did not add where "here" was. There was a great shadow, which possibly did duty for a house, but, if so, there was not a light in any of the windows, and there was nothing visible in the shape of a door. The whereabouts of this, however, the driver presently made clear.

"There be the door in front of you; you go up three steps, if you can find 'em. There's a knocker, if none of 'em haven't twisted it off. If they have, there's a bell on your right, if it isn't broken."

There appeared to be no knocker, though whether it had been "twisted" off was more that I could say. But there was a bell, which creaked with rust, though it was not broken. I heard it tinkle in the distance. No answer; though I allowed a more than decent interval.

"Better ring again," suggested the driver. "Hard. Maybe they're up to some of their games and wants rousing."

Was there a chuckle in the fellow's voice? I rang again and again with all the force I could. The bell reverberated through what seemed like an empty house.

"Is there no one in the place?"

"They're there, right enough. Where's another thing. Maybe

on the roof, or in the cellar. If they know you're coming, perhaps they hear and don't choose to answer. Better ring again."

I sounded another peal. Presently feet were heard advancing along the passage—several pairs, it seemed—and a light gleamed though the window over the door. A voice inquired.

"Who's there?"

"Mr. Christopher from London."

The information was greeted with what sounded uncomfortably like a chorus of laughter. There was a rush of retreating feet, an expostulating voice, then darkness again, and silence.

"Who lives here? Are the people mad?"

"Well, thereabouts."

Once more I suspected the driver of a chuckle. My temper was rising. I had not come all that way, and subjected myself to so much discomfort, to be played tricks with. I tolled the bell again.

After a few seconds' interval, the pit-pat of what was obviously one pair of feet came toward the door. Again a light gleamed through the pane. A key was turned, a chain unfastened, bolts withdrawn; it seemed as if someone had to drag a chair forward before one of these latter could be reached. After a vast amount of unfastening, the door was opened, and on the threshold there stood a girl with a lighted candle in her hand. The storm rushed in, she put up her hand to shield the light from danger.

"Can I see Mrs. Wilson? I'm expected. I'm Mr. Christopher, from London."

"Oh!"

That was all she said. I looked at her; she at me. The driver's voice came in from the background.

"I drove him over from the station, Miss. There be a lot of luggage. He do say he's come to stay with you."

"Is that you, Tidy? I'm afraid I can offer you nothing to drink. We've lost the key of the cellar, and there's nothing except water, and I don't think you'd care for that."

"I can't say rightly as how I should, Miss. Next time will do. Be it all right?" The girl continued to regard me.

"Perhaps you had better come inside."

"I think I had."

I went inside; it was time.

"Have you any luggage?" I admitted that I had.

"Perhaps it had better be brought in."

"Perhaps it had."

"Do you think that you could manage, Tidy?"

"The mare, she'll stand still enough, I should think I could, Miss."

By degrees my belongings were borne into the hall, hidden under an envelope of snow. The driver was paid, the cart disappeared, the door was shut; the girl and I were alone together.

"We didn't expect that you would come."

"Not expect me? But it was all arranged; I wrote to say that I should come. Did you not receive my letter?"

"We thought that you were joking."

"Joking! Why should you imagine that?"

"We were joking."

"You were? Then I am to gather that I have been made the subject of a practical joke, and that I am an intruder?"

"Well, it's quite true that we did not think you were in earnest. You see, it's this way: we're alone."

"Alone? Who are 'we'?"

"Well, it would take a good while to explain, and you look tired and cold."

"I am both."

"Perhaps you're hungry?"

"I am."

"I don't know what you can have to eat, unless it's tomorrow's dinner."

"Tomorrow's dinner!" I stared. "Can I see Mrs. Wilson?"

"Mrs. Wilson? That's Mamma. She's dead."

"I beg your pardon. Can I see your father?"

"Oh, Father's been dead for years."

"Then to whom have I the pleasure of speaking?"

"I'm Madge. I'm Mother now."

"You are—Mother now?"

"The trouble will be where you are to sleep—unless it's with the boys. The rooms are all topsy-turvy, and I'm sure I don't know where the beds are."

"I suppose there are servants in the house."

"No. The boys thought they were nuisances, so we got rid of them. The last went yesterday. She wouldn't do any work so we thought she'd better go."

"Under those circumstances, I think you were right. Then am I to understand that there are children?"

"Rather!"

As she spoke there came a burst of laughter from the other end of the passage. I spun around. No one was in sight.

"They're waiting around the corner. Perhaps we'd better have them here. You people, you better come and let me introduce you to Mr. Christopher."

A procession of boys and girls began to appear from around the corner. In front was a girl of about sixteen. She advanced with outstretched hand and an air of self-possession which took me at a disadvantage.

"I'm Bessie. I'm sorry we kept you waiting at the door, but the fact is that we thought it was Eliza's brother who had come to insult us again."

"Pray, don't mention it. I am glad that it was not Eliza's brother."

"So am I. He is a dreadful man."

I shook hands with the rest of them. There were six more: four boys and two girls. They formed a considerable congregation as they stood eyeing me with inquiring eyes. Madge was the first to speak.

"I wondered all along if he would take it as a joke, and you see he hasn't. I thought it was a risky thing to do."

"I like that! You keep your thoughts to yourself then. It was you who proposed it. You said you'd been reading about some-

thing of the kind in a story, and you voted for advertising ourselves for a lark."

The speaker was the biggest boy, a good-looking youngster
with sallow cheeks and shrewd black eyes.

"But, Rupert, I never meant it to go so far as this."

"How far did you mean it to go, then? It was your idea all
through. You sent in the advertisement, you wrote the letters,
and now he's here. If you didn't mean it, why didn't you stop
his coming?"

"Rupert!"

The girl's cheeks were crimson. Bessie interposed.

"The thing is, that, as he is here, it's no good worrying about
whose fault it is. We shall simply have to make the best of it."
Then to me, "I suppose you really have come to stay?"

"I confess that I had some notion of the kind—to spend an
old-fashioned Christmas." At this, there was laughter, chiefly
from the boys. Rupert exclaimed:

"A nice sort of old-fashioned Christmas you'll find it will be.
You'll be sorry you came before it's through."

"I am not so sure of that."

There appeared to be something in my tone which caused a
touch of silence to descend upon the group. They regarded each
other doubtfully, as if in my words a reproof were implied. Bess
was again the spokeswoman.

"Of course, now that you have come, we mean to be nice to
you—that is, as nice as we can. Because the thing is that we're
not in a condition to receive visitors. Do we look as if we were?"

To be frank, they did not. Even Madge was a little unkempt, while the boys were in what I believe is the state of the average boy.

"And," murmured Madge, "where is Mr. Christopher to sleep?"

"What is he to eat?" inquired Bessie. She glanced at my packages. "I suppose you have brought nothing with you?"

"I'm afraid I haven't. I had hoped to find something ready for me."

Again they peeped at each other as if ashamed. Madge repeated her former suggestion.

"There's tomorrow's dinner."

"Oh, hang it!" exclaimed Robert. "It's not as bad as that. There's a ham."

"Uncooked."

"You can cut a steak off, or whatever you call it, and have it broiled."

A meal was got ready, in the preparation of which every member of the family took a hand. And a room was found for me in which were a blazing fire and traces of recent feminine occupation. I suspected that Madge had yielded her own apartment as a shelter for the stranger. By the time I had washed and changed my clothes the impromptu dinner, or supper, or whatever it was, was ready.

A curious repast it proved to be, composed of oddly contrasted dishes cooked—and sometimes uncooked—in original fashion. But hunger, that piquant sauce, gave it a relish of its

own. But no one seemed disposed to join me. By degrees, however, one after another found a knife and fork, until all the eight
were seated with me around the board eating, some of them, as
if for dear life.

"The fact is," explained Rupert, "we're a rum lot. We hardly
ever sit down together. We don't have regular meals, but whenever any one feels peckish he goes and gets what there is and
cooks it and eats it on his own hook!"

"It's not as bad as that," protested Madge, "though it's pretty
bad."

It did seem pretty bad from the conventional point of view.
From their conversation, which was candor itself, I gleaned de-
tails which threw light on the peculiar position of affairs. It
seemed that their father had been dead some seven years. Their
mother, who had always been delicate, had allowed them to run
nearly wild. Since she died, some ten months back, they appeared to have run quite wild. The house, with some six hundred acres of land, was theirs, and an income as to whose exact
amount no one seemed quite clear.

"It's about eight hundred a year," said Rupert.

"I don't think it's quite so much," doubted Madge.

"I'm sure it's more," declared Bessie. "I believe we're being
robbed."

I thought it extremely probable. They must have had peculiar parents. Their father had left everything absolutely to their
mother, and their mother in her turn everything in trust to
Madge, to be shared equally among them all. Madge was an

odd trustee. In her hands the household had become a republic in which everyone did exactly as he or she pleased.

The result was chaos. No one wanted to go to school, so no one went. The servants, finding themselves provided with eight masters and mistresses, followed their example and did as they liked. Consequently, after sundry battles royal—lively episodes some of them had evidently been—one after the other had been got rid of until now not one remained. Plainly the house must be going to rack and ruin.

"But you have no relatives?" I inquired.

Rupert answered.

"We've got some cousins or uncles, or something of the kind, in Australia, where, so far as I'm concerned, I hope they'll stop."

When I was in my room, which I feared was Madge's, I told myself that it was a queer establishment on which I had alighted. Yet I could not honestly affirm that I was sorry I had come. I had lived such an uneventful and such a solitary life, and had so often longed for someone in whom to take an interest, that to be plunged all at once into the center of this troop of boys and girls was an accident which, if only because of its novelty, I found amusing. And then it was so odd that I should have come across a Madge at last!

In the morning I was aroused by noises the cause of which at first I could not understand. By degrees, the explanation dawned on me. The family was putting the house to rights. A somewhat noisy process, it seemed. Someone was singing, someone else was shouting, and two or three others were engaged in a heated argument. In such loud tones was it conducted that the gist of the matter traveled up to me.

"How do you think I'm going to get this fire to burn if you beastly kids keep messing it about? It's no good banging at it with a poker until it's alight."

The voice was unmistakably Rupert's. There was the sound of a scuffle, cries of indignation, then a girlish voice pouring oil upon the troubled waters. Presently there was a rattle and clatter as if someone had fallen from the top of the house to the bottom. I rushed to my bedroom door.

"What on earth has happened?"

A small boy was outside—Peter. He explained:

"Oh, it's only the broom and the dustpan gone tobogganing down the stairs. It's Bessie's fault; she shouldn't leave them on the landing."

Bessie appeared from the room opposite, disclaimed responsibility.

"I told you to look where you were going, but you never do. I'd only put them down for a second, while I went in to empty a jug of water onto Jack, who won't get out of bed, and there are all the boots for him to clean."

Injured tones came through the open portal.

"You wait, that's all. I'll soak your bed tonight—I'll drown it. I don't want to clean your dirty boots. I'm not a shoeblack."

The breakfast was a failure. To begin with, it was inordinately late. It seemed that a bath was not obtainable. I had been promised some hot water, but as I waited and waited and none arrived I proceeded to break the ice in my jug—it was a bitterly cold morning; nice "old-fashioned" weather—and to wash in the half-frozen contents. As I am not accustomed to performing my ablutions in partially dissolved ice, I fear that the process did not improve my temper.

It was past eleven when I got down, feeling not exactly in a Christmassy frame of mind. Everything and everyone seemed at sixes and sevens. It was after noon when breakfast appeared. The principal dish consisted of eggs and bacon; but as the bacon was fried to cinders and the eggs were all broken, it was not so popular as it might have been. Madge was moved to melancholy.

"Something will have to be done! We can't go on like this! We must have someone in to help us!"

Bessie was sarcastic.

"You might give Eliza another trial. She told you if you didn't like the way she burned the bacon, to burn it yourself, and as you've followed her advice she might be able to give you other useful hints on similar lines."

Rupert indulged himself in the same vein.

"Then there's Eliza's brother. He threatened to knock your blooming head off for saying Eliza was dishonest just because she collared everything she could lay her hands on; he might turn out a useful creature to have about the place."

"It's all very well for you to laugh, but it's beyond a jest. I don't know how we're going to cook the dinner."

"Can I be of any assistance?" I inquired. "First of all, what is there to cook?"

It seemed that there were a good many things to cook. A turkey, a goose, beef, plum pudding, mince pies, custard, sardines—it seemed that Molly, the third girl, as she phrased it, could "live on sardines" and esteemed no dinner a decent dinner at which they did not appear—together with a list of etceteras half as long as my arm.

"One thing is clear, you can't cook all these things today."

"We can't cook anything."

This was Rupert. He was tilting his chair back, and had his face turned toward the ceiling.

"Why not?"

"Because there's no coal."

"No coal?"

"There's about half a scuttleful of dust. If you can make it burn you'll be clever."

What Rupert said was correct. Madge confessed, with crimson cheeks, that she had meant, over and over again, to order some coal, but had continually forgotten about it until finally Christmas Day had found them with an empty cellar. There was plenty of wood, but it was not so dry as it might have been, and the grate was not constructed to burn wood.

I began to rub my chin. Considering the breakfast we had had, from my point of view, the situation commenced to look really grave. I wondered if it would not be possible to take the whole eight somewhere where something really eatable could be gotten. But when I broached the subject I learned that the thing could not be done. The nearest hostelry was the Boy and Blunderbuss, and it was certain that nothing eatable could be had there, even if accommodation could be found for us at all. Nothing in the shape of a house of public entertainment was to be found closer than the market town, eight miles off; it was unlikely that even there a Christmas dinner for nine could be provided at a moment's notice. Evidently the only thing to do was to make the best of things.

When the meeting broke up, Madge came and said a few words to me alone.

"I really think that you had better not stay."

"Does that mean that you had rather I went?"

"No; not exactly that."

"Then nearly that?"

"No; not a bit that. Only that you must see for yourself how awfully uncomfortable you'll be here."

"My dear Madge"—everybody called her Madge, so I did—"even if I wanted to go, which I don't—and I would remind you that you contracted to give me an old-fashioned Christmas—I don't see where there is that I could go."

"Of course, there's that. I don't see, either. So I suppose you'll have to stay. But I hope you won't think that I meant you to come to a place like this—really, you know."

"I'm sorry; I had hoped you had."

"That's not what I mean. I mean that if I had expected you, I would have seen that things were different."

"How different? I assure you that things as they are have a charm of their own."

"That's what you say. You don't suppose that I'm so silly as not to know you're laughing at me? But as I am the whole cause of your coming, I hope you won't hate the others because of me."

That Christmas dinner was a success—positively—of a kind; let it be clearly understood. I am not implying that it was a success from the point of view of a *chef de cuisine*. Not at all; how could it be? Quite the other way. By dint of ransacking all the rooms and emptying all the scuttles we collected a certain amount of coal, with which, after adding a fair proportion of wood, we managed—not brilliantly, but after a fashion.

I can only say, personally, that I had not enjoyed myself so much for years. I really felt as if I were young again; I am not sure that I am not younger than I thought I was. I must look the matter up. And, after all, even if one be, say, forty, one need not be absolutely an ancient. Madge herself said that I had been like a right hand to her; she did not know what she would have done without me.

Looking back, I cannot but think that if we had attempted to prepare fewer dishes something might have been properly cooked. It was a mistake to stuff the turkey with sage and onions; but as Bessie did not discover that she had been manipulating the wrong bird until the process of stuffing had been completed, it was felt that we might just as well let it rest. Unfortunately it turned out that some thyme, parsley, mint and other things had got mixed with the sage, which gave the creature quite a peculiar flavor; but as it came to the table nearly raw, and as tough as hickory, it really did not matter.

My experience of that day teaches me that it is not easy to roast a large goose on a small oil stove. The dropping fat caused the flame to give out a strong-smelling and most unpleasant smoke. Rupert, who had charge of the operation, affirmed that it would be all right in the end. But by the time the thing was served it was as black as my hat. Rupert said that it was merely brown, but the brown was of a sooty hue. We had to have it deposited in the ash bin.

I dare say that the beef would have not been bad if some one had occasionally turned it, and if the fire had burned clear. As it was, it was charred on one side and raw on the other and smoked all over. The way in which the odor and taste of smoke permeated everything was amazing. The plum pudding came to the table in the form of a soup, and the mince pies were nauseous.

Luckily we came on a tin of corned beef in a cupboard, and with the aid of some bread and cheese and other odds and ends we made a sort of picnic. Incredible though it may seem, I enjoyed it. If there was anywhere a merrier party than we were I should like to know where it was to be found. When I produced the presents, in which a happy inspiration had urged me to invest, the enthusiasm reached a climax.

That was my first introduction to the "lively family." They came up to the description they had given of themselves. I speak from knowledge, for they have been my acquaintances now some time—more than acquaintances: friends; the dearest friends I have. At their request I took their affairs in hand, Madge informally passing her trusteeship on to me. Things are very different with them now. The house is spick-and-span. There is an excellent staff of servants. Hangar Dene is as comfortable a home as there is in England. I have spent many a Christmas under its roof.

The boys are out in the world, after passing with honor through school and college. The girls are going out into the world also. Bessie is actually married. Madge is married too. She is Mrs. Christopher. That is the part of it all which I find the hardest to understand—to have told myself that the name of my ideal woman would be Madge and to have won that woman for my own at last! I thought that I was beyond all that kind of thing—that I was too old. But Madge seemed to think that I was young enough. And now there is a little Madge, who is big enough to play havoc with the sheets of paper on which I have been scribbling.

# "In the Toy Shop"

FROM *THE SATURDAY EVENING POST*, DECEMBER 25, 1897

F.G.T.

Ours was a small German village, which boasted of but a single shop. This was not very attractive in appearance, but of the usual kind, small, low, and dark, with gas in the one window, that was anything but bright, and a doorway that was anything but a lofty one.

In the window there was usually a plateful of rosy-cheeked apples, near to a heap of nuts, two or three jars of sweets, making a tempting display to the little folks, while a few lemons, tapes, buttons and pins completed the display. Inside the shop good old Mrs. Hollyberry kept a very small stock of useful things required by her neighbors, who were as poor as herself.

But when this Christmas Eve came, there was a grand transformation. The window was cleaned, and Mrs. Hollyberry removed all the tapes, buttons and pins, and filled their place with toys of the most wonderful description.

There were brilliant red dogs, looking as fierce as lions; black cats, with two wide yellow stripes down their backs; brown and dappled-gray horses on wheels with stiff hairy tails standing straight out; dolls clothed in marvelous costumes; boxes of tin and wooden soldiers; mewing cats, tops, penny trumpets, tea sets; and, in short, toys of all kinds.

There never had been such a gorgeous display of toys in the village before, and their gay colors shone forth in happy contrast with the snow that covered the ground and roofs, until they looked as if they were bearing great white pillows on their heads.

Everybody stopped to look at Mrs. Hollyberry's window; it was the one event in the village. But the children stood before it the whole day long, with their feet cooling in the melting snow, their ears crimson with the cold, and their hands thrust into their pockets, or under their cloaks and shawls. Even when it grew dark, they still lingered, knowing that Mrs. Hollyberry would be sure to light her lamp, and then the toys would look prettier than ever.

Finally the lamp hanging from the ceiling was lighted, and a brilliant glow was sent over the toys and fruit in the window. The children pressed up closer and closer, coughing, sneezing, chattering and continually stamping their feet to keep them warm.

The toys seemed to feel their importance, and were as proud and pleased—those common little toys—as the finest wax dolls and the largest rocking horses in any large shop in a town. They looked out on the little round faces lighted up by Mrs. Hollyberry's lamp, and thought what a pretty sight they made.

Meanwhile the boys and girls gazed on, until their mothers appeared at the open doors of their houses, and suddenly put an end to their pleasures by calling them in to bed.

Slowly they went off, one or two at a time, with many backward glances, the last of all having gently licked the glass in front with his tongue to clear away the vapor, which concealed the largest and most tempting of all the horses from his view.

Soon the children were all safe in bed. Then the mothers started out with their baskets in their hands to the shop, where the toys were still looking out for purchasers.

Mrs. Hollyberry showed her toys one by one, and the mothers made their choice and paid her, some with silver and others with very worn and battered copper coins, and all went away with one or more toys.

By degrees the dolls disappeared from the window, until at last only two were left, but they were so dear that no one could be persuaded to buy them. Then came the turn of the tin and wooden soldiers, and the brave little fellows, as they rolled to the bottoms of the baskets, felt as if drilling was at the end for them, and they were all commanders-in-chief at last, and decorated with medals and ribbons all over their little chests.

The gingerbread, apples, nuts and oranges also found their way into the baskets, and left empty plates behind them; the bottles of sweets, all new this evening, were now only half full, and almost the only toys that remained to keep company with the dolls were a donkey with a pair of packs and a nodding head, a beautiful wooden horse with a red saddle and a bridle, a barking dog, a cat with a group of little kittens, a drum, and a dancing Punch puppet.

All these toys were too costly for Mrs. Hollyberry's customers, and she shut the door on the last of them and shook her head mournfully, put up the shutters and went to bed to dream of the squire coming in a carriage and four to buy up all the toys she had left.

The shop was quiet now, and all the toys commenced to dream. The cat imagined that it was purring in front of a hot fire, and at the same time, scratching up a tender little mouse; the dog dreamed he was gnawing a delicious bone, and the dolls dreamed sweetly of the deft little hands of girls dressing and undressing them, and giving tea parties in their honor.

The rejected toys had dreamed as sweet as those that had been carried off in the baskets, but Christmas Eve is the time when they speak and move; they throw off their coverings of cardboard and wood, and although for all the rest of the year, they are motionless, sleepy and speechless, when midnight comes on that one night, they rouse up and are alive at once.

When the bells at midnight sang out, "Ding-dong, ding-dong," gently, for fear of rousing the children, no words can express the delighted happiness of the toys.

The trumpets were seized with a sudden fit of gaiety, and blew long blasts; the cats squeezed their own bellows, and mewed Christmas greetings to each other; the dolls shook out their skirts, and curtseyed; the dogs and horses sang carols together, and the donkeys joined in the chorus; even the tea sets rattled pleasantly as they shook themselves free of their boxes and took their places to dance a quadrille with the dinner sets. There was not a toy in the village that did not come to life, and show its happiness in some manner or other.

Old Mrs. Hollyberry heard nothing of all this. She was wrapped up snugly under the blankets, and never dreamed that toys could dance and sing as they were then doing on the counter of her little shop, and in nearly every cottage in the village. But not in all, for in some, the fathers and mothers were too poor to be able to buy even the cheapest toys for their children.

But, although Mrs. Hollyberry had been sound asleep, oddly, she could see as well as she had ever seen in her life, and what she saw was this:

The shop door opened, and Santa Claus walked in and gathered in his arms all the pretty but expensive toys that had been left in her shop because no one could afford to buy them.

Mrs. Hollyberry was not a bit astonished or angry, and only said to herself, "Nothing is too expensive for Santa Claus: he dearly loves good children, and is sure to leave the money in my drawer."

When he had collected all the toys, she saw him enter his sleigh and skim rapidly over the snow-covered ground, stopping at the cottages where there were no toys for the children, dropping gently down each chimney a toy for each child, not one being forgotten.

When Mrs. Hollyberry awoke she remembered what she had seen in the night and was pleased to think that the very poorest children would have the nicest toys, and she was not at all frightened about her money, as indeed she had no reason to be, for when she looked in the drawer, she found that Santa Claus had paid her honestly for all the toys he had taken to give away.

But who can tell the surprise and delight of the children and their parents at the unexpected gifts? The parents knew their children had been remembered by Santa Claus himself; the children did not question where the toys came from, and it was the happiest and merriest Christmas they had ever spent, for never before had they had such beautiful presents given to them.

# "Celia's Happy Christmas"

FROM THE *NEW YORK DAILY TRIBUNE*, SUNDAY, DECEMBER 22, 1901

## What the Spirit of Love and Goodwill Brought to a Little Girl

Little Celia was thinking of the merry Christmas so near, and wondering what she could do to make it as happy a time to others as she knew it would be to her. Her home was lovely and luxurious, but her kind little heart was heavy for the poor children of the settlement where lived "the millhands," who were out of work because the mills were shut down on account of the hard times.

It did not seem easy to plan any way to help them, for her pocket money would not go far toward getting a beautiful tree full of toys, as she longed to do. So she climbed to her playroom in the turret to "think it over" by herself.

The sun was streaming into the room, and Celia sat with her chubby face resting on her dimpled hands and watched the dancing rays. Presently a strange thing happened. One ray grew brighter and brighter, and a tiny form came tripping down the stream of light. It was a radiant creature in white and gold, with gauzy wings that changed in the sunlight until they seemed to reflect all the colors of the rainbow. Crowning the beautiful flowing tresses of her hair was a jewel that glistened with such splendor that it was only possible to gaze at it for a moment. In her right hand the figure held a wand, surmounted by one bright star.

"This must be one of the fairies of the mountain," thought Celia, and after gazing for some minutes in silent admiration at this charming little creature she whispered, "Who are you?"

"I am the Christmastide Spirit of Love and Goodwill," came the reply in a voice that sounded like the sweetest chime of bells.

"And why have you come to me?" asked Celia.

"I always come to those who forget self in trying to make others happy," said the Spirit. "When all is still tonight and the moon is shining I shall come here for you, and together we will visit the homes you wish to brighten." And with a wave of the wand she vanished.

When the shadows of evening had lengthened into the night and the quiet moonlight rested on the snow, Celia hurried to her turret room and opened one of windows just in time to see a white swan appear bearing on his back a golden throne large enough for two, and on this the Spirit was seated. With a silent motion the Spirit pointed to the place beside her, and as Celia seated herself the swan bore them swiftly away from the home of wealth to the settlement where Christmas meant so little.

As they descended in front of the first hut the door swung slowly open, and Celia noticed that although there was no lamp, a soft glow filled the room. Peering in, Celia saw that a sick child lay dozing on the bed, and the father, who wore his rough laborer's clothes, was asleep in a chair at the bedside of his child, whose hand he held.

"What makes this poor room light when there is no lamp or candle?" asked Celia.

"It is never wholly dark where love abounds," answered the Spirit. "That father's greatest happiness is in his affection for his child, and it brightens even his poverty."

From door to door they flitted. Celia could recognize the homes where there was love, for no matter how poor or unhappy the people might be, the soft light was there.

"Now, I am going to tell you how you may bring Christmas joy into every home we have visited," said the Spirit, as they stepped from the golden throne into the turret room. "Under that old bureau is a secret hiding place, where some papers were hidden long ago, and there you will find enough gold to do all the good work you had planned." And with a friendly wave of the hand the Spirit vanished from the room.

The next day, when her father visited Celia's playroom, they took apart the old bureau, just for fun, as they had often done before, and there in the secret compartment lay the gold.

"Whatever sum this compartment holds shall be yours to do with as you like," said her father, and Celia's thoughts flew to the darkened lives of the settlement.

"Then I wish to spend it in giving a real Christmas to those who have never known one," said Celia.

The next few days were busy ones for Celia, as she drove from store to store, buying turkeys and provisions and the prettiest toys she could find.

When Christmas came there was feasting in every home of the settlement, and in the town hall was a huge tree hung with gifts for every poor person in the village.

The day after Christmas, as Celia sat in her turret room watching the sunlight dance across the floor, she murmured to herself. "I never spent such a happy Christmas before, and I wonder if I shall ever see that beautiful Spirit again."

Then at once there was a bright light and the Spirit came gliding down the sunbeam.

"Oh!" said Celia, softly, "I feared you had forgotten me, and perhaps now you have come to say goodby."

"We need never say goodby, unless you wish it," replied the Spirit. "My home will be with you as long as you let me stay. I, and others like me, sometimes make a long and weary search before we find homes where we can breathe the message of love and goodwill that the Christ child of Bethlehem brought hundreds of years ago. Many refuse to hear our message, and others say it is only meant for Christmas time; yet when we have gone, they know that the best thing in life has departed."

"Then stay with me always," said Celia. "Make your home in my heart, and let me constantly hear your message of love."

"Although you will not see me, you will know when I am with you," replied the Spirit, who slowly began to fade into the sunlight. "Every time that you feel a throb of pity for the suffering and follow the impulse to do a kindly act you will know that the Spirit of Love and Goodwill dwells in your heart, and is calling to you, and in following her teachings, you will find a happiness that nothing else in this world can give, and that nothing can take away."

At the last word the Spirit faded out of sight, but the ray of light in which she had stood remained. And Celia, gazing at it, whispered over and over to herself, "Good Spirit, I shall strive day by day to hold your teachings in my heart."

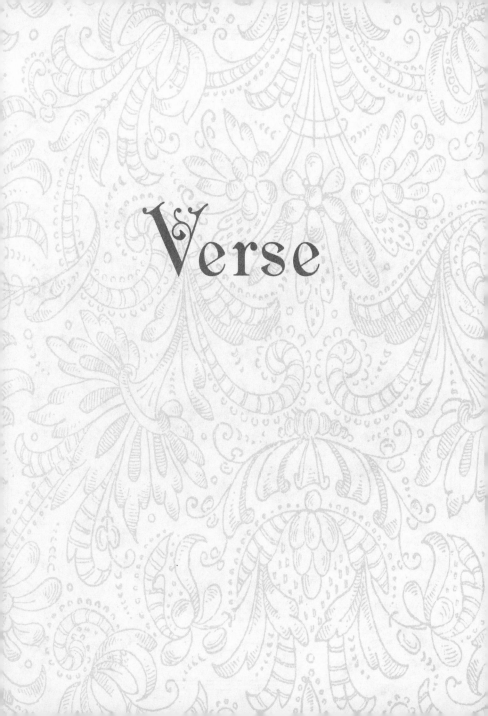

# Verse

# "Signs of Christmas"

When Ma begins to tiptoe round
   'N' we begin to hear
A certain husky, whisp'rin' sound
   About this time of year,
We know that she and Santy Claus
   Are fixin' things to do,
'N' so we never peek, because
   They never want us to.
When Sister Mary goes about
   A-hinting that she wishes
She had a teapot with a spout
   To match her set of dishes,
We know its time for us to write
   Our letter 'n' to set 'em
Beside the hearth where, in the night,
   Ole Santy Claus'll get 'em.
When all the seats in Sunday school
   Are filled 'ith girls 'n' boys
'N' no one ever breaks a rule
   'R makes a bit of noise,
We know it can't be very long
   Till Santy will appear

'N' pass his presents to the throng
  That comes but once a year.
When Aunt Melindy comes 'n' brings
  The children 'n' the bird
'N' she 'n' Ma make popcorn strings,
  We never say a word.
But anybody ought to see
  That she has come to stay
Till time to have the Chris'mus tree,
  Which can't be far away.
When Pa comes sneakin' 'crost the lot
  A-lookin' guilty, so't
You'd think he's stole the things he's got
  Inside his overcoat,
We know it's times for us to run
  'N' carry in the wood
'N' see that all our chores are done
  'N' otherwise be good.

# "Santa Claus's Petition"

Dear Children—I write in great haste to say:
I've met with an accident coming this way.
As Christmas is near, and I've so much to do,
I really must beg a slight favor of you;
And, unless I mistake, the small folks of this nation
Will spare poor old Santa great mortification
By setting about with their might and their main
To see that the accident's righted again.
You know, I suppose, that the distance is great
I travel each year; and for fear I'll be late,
I whip up my reindeer, and make each good steed
Go prancing along at the top of his speed.
This year my big sleigh was as full as 't could hold;
I wrapped me up warm—for the weather was cold—
And started once more on my gay Christmas tour
With the lightest of hearts, you may be very sure.
Hi! How the bells jingled and mingled in tune!
I bowed to the stars and winked to the moon.
I found myself crossing the great open sea,
With dolphins and merchildren gazing at me;
I bent a bit over the side of my sleigh
To wave them a hand, when—ah! me lackaday!—

A stocking crammed full to the very small toe
Fell over the back to the sea down below.
And there the merchildren made merry ado
With toys I had meant for some dear one of you.
So this is my accident and I would ask—
I know you won't deem it a troublesome task—
That is, should you see some poor child with no toys
Upon Christmas morning, dear girls and dear boys,
You'll know the fat stocking he was to have had
Is deep in the sea, and poor Santa is sad,
And see that the accident's righted, because
'Twill be a great favor to

Yours,
Santa Claus

# "From a Little Girl"

I've written this letter to Santa,
   To tell him our chimney is high,
I'm sure he could not come down it,
   So, really, there's no use to try.
Now, Santa, just ring at the door bell,
   I'll listen far into the night,
And let you in quickly and softly,
   I'll bring you my own little light.

## "From a Little Boy"

Oh, dear, oh, dear, what can I do,
　　With Christmas Day so near!
I'm looking out for Santa Claus,
　　With his snowy, white reindeer.
I know he'll drive them on the roof,
　　And try to scramble down
Our great tall chimney—but, oh, then!
　　How Santa Claus will frown!
For we have but a big coal stove,
　　And not a fireplace;
So Santa'll mark me off his list,
　　With scowls upon his face.
But I have thought what I can do:
　　I'll take my stocking up
And nail it to the chimney top,
　　Then he can fill it up.

# "When Santa Claus Is President"

When Santa Claus is President,
    What good times there will be!
Then every bush beside the door
    May be a "Christmas tree."
Then dolls, and skates, and kites, and sleds,
    We'll have the whole year round,
And never have to wait for them
    Till snow is on the ground.
Then Grandma'll be vice-president,
    And Uncle John—why, he—
Perhaps he'll be the cabinet,
    To help around, you see,
For Santa will have lots to do,
    And need so many sleighs
And carts to carry presents round
    So many, many days.
I wish they'd let the children vote;
    I'm sure we'd put them in—
The good times that they tell about
    would right away begin.
Our country's in a dreadful state,
    With ruin very near;

But if Santa Claus were president,
He'll save us all, 'tis clear.

## "When Daddy Lights the Tree"

We have our share of ups and downs,
  Our cares like other folk;
The pocketbook is sometimes full,
  We're sometimes nigh dead broke;
But once a year at Christmastime
  Our hearth is bright to see;
The baby's hand just touches heaven
  When Daddy lights the tree.
For weeks and weeks the little ones
  Have counted on this hour;
And mother, she has planned for it
  Since summer's sun and shower,
With here a nickel, there a dime,
  Put by where none should see,
A loving hoard against the night
  When Daddy lights the tree.
The tiny tapers glow like stars;
  They 'mind us of the flame
That rifted once the steel-blue sky
  The morn the Christ child came;
The blessed angels sang to earth
  Above that far countree,

We think they sing above our hearth
    When Daddy lights the tree.
The west kid in Mother's arms,
    Laughs out and claps her hands,
The rest of us on tiptoe wait,
    The grown-up brother stands
Where he can reach the topmost branch,
    Our Santa Claus to be,
In that sweet hour of breathless joy
    When Daddy lights the tree.

Our grandpa says 'twas just as fine
    In days when he was young;
For every Christmas ages through
    The happy bells have rung.
And Daddy's head is growing gray,
    But yet a boy is he,
As merry as the rest of us
    When Daddy lights the tree.
'Tis Love that makes the world go round,
    'Tis Love that lightens toil,
'Tis Love that lays up treasure which
    Nor moth nor rust can spoil;

And Love is in our humble home,
  In largesse full and free,
We all are very close to heaven
  When Daddy lights the tree.

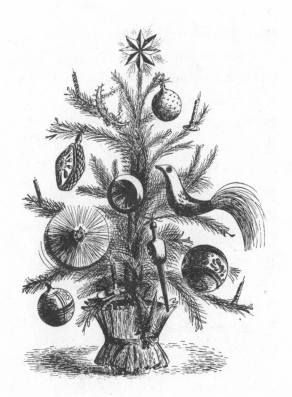

# "Christmas Letters"

(FROM SIX CHILDREN.)

Thomas Bailey Aldrich


Dear Santa Claus, I write to you
To tell you what to bring—
I want a little knife and fork,
And a silver napkin ring.
Dear Santa Claus, I write to you
That you may surely know
I'd like to have a train of cars,
With an engine that will go.
Dear Santa Claus, when you come down,
You'll find my stocking there—
I'd like to have a picture book,
And a little rocking chair.
Dear Santa Claus, now when you come,
I'd like best of all
To have a bat and baseball glove,
And a very hard baseball.
Dear Santa Claus, please will you bring
To baby and to me—
We want it, oh, so very much!—
A real Christmas tree.

48

Dear Santa Claus, not much I'll ask,
For I am very small,
I only want a horse and cart,
And a drum, a horn and ball.

(LET EACH STANZA BE RECITED BY CHILD WITH LETTER IN HIS HAND.)

49

FROM *THE TWENTIETH CENTURY CHRISTMAS EXERCISES* BY GEORGE OTIS MARCH, LEBANON, OH: MARCH BROTHERS PUBLISHERS, 1903.

# "Kriss Kringle"

Just as the moon was fading
   Amid her misty rings,
And every stocking was stuffed
   With childhood's precious things,
Old Kriss Kringle looked round,
   And saw on the elm-tree bough,
High-hung, an oriole's nest,
   Silent and empty now.
"Quite like a stocking," he laughed,
   "Pinned up there on a tree!
Little I thought the birds
   Expected a present from me!"
Then old Kriss Kringle, who loves
   A joke as well as the best,
Dropped a handful of flakes
   In the oriole's empty nest.

THE BOOK OF CHRISTMAS. WITH AN INTRODUCTION BY HAMILTON MABIE. NEW YORK: MACMILLAN, 1909.

# Untitled
Albert Bigelow Paine

"When the turkey's on the table
An' the mince pie's on the way,
An' my plate is filled with fixin's
That belong to Christmas Day,
I fergit I'm over eighty
An' about my rheumatiz,
An' it seems to me that livin'
Is the best thing that there is."

51

MY CHRISTMAS GIFT: A LITTLE BOOK OF CHRISTMAS THOUGHTS.
EDITED BY EDWIN OSGOOD GROVER. CHICAGO: P.F. VOLLAND
& CO., 1912.

# "His First and Last Christmas"

Trim the Old Year a Christmas tree,
He'll not be with us very long,
Make his last week a merry one,
With laughter, dancing, and with song.
His tastes are fine, and you all know,
That Pinaud's Perfumes suit him well.
Let's give him some of every kind,
Which he loves best we none can tell.
A bottle of Pinaud's Tonique,
And one of Extrait Vegetal,
And all the perfumes Pinaud makes,
At Christmas time, give him we shall.
Perhaps to others, ere he dies,
These treasures he may give away,
Give to the friends he loves the best,
In memory of this happy day.
Mid blossoms sweet, his head laid low,
The Old Year lies, his work all done,
His Christmas gifts from Ed Pinaud,
Left to the heir, young Nineteen-One.

THE NEW YORK DAILY TRIBUNE, DECEMBER 1900

# "Modern Santa Claus"

## Arthur H. Folwell

Said Santa Claus on Christmas Eve:
"No more mankind should I deceive,
A fact it is I've changed my ways,
Abandoned deer, attached to sleighs,
And substituted methods new
To rush my Christmas business through.
Pneumatic tubes comprise my plan,
Inventions of ingenious man,
Which take my goods at Christmastime
To young and old in every clime.
No longer need I harness up,
With scarcely time for stirrup cup,
And speed my yearly Christmas quest,
With ne'er a chance to pause or rest.
My reindeer drowse in cozy stall,
My furs hang high on yonder wall,
While I, reposing snugly here,
May rest, yet keep my conscience clear.
My faithful agents, wisely placed,
Distribute now where once I raced.
Don't blame me, please, for what I've done;

53

The change won't injure anyone.
It simply shows a natural fate,
That Santa Claus is up-to-date."

*THE BROOKLYN DAILY EAGLE, DECEMBER 23, 1900*

# "The Children's Time"

## K.C.

Christmas is the children's time;
Make them happy then.
Make them gladly welcome it
When it comes again.
Christmas is the children's time;
We of older years
See the light of Christmastide
Through a mist of tears.
Christmas is the children's time;
'Tis the birthday feast
Of the Child whose star once led
Wise men from the East.
And let us, at Christmastide,
Do our best to make
All the little ones be glad
For the Child's dear sake.

55

THE SATURDAY EVENING POST, DECEMBER 25, 1897

# "The Night After Christmas"
## By Anne P.L. Field

'Twas the night after Christmas in Santa-Claus land
And to rest from his labors St. Nicholas planned.
The reindeer were turned out to pasture and all
The ten thousand assistants discharged till the fall.
The furry greatcoat was laid safely away
With the boots and the cap with its tassel so gay,
And toasting his toes by a merry wood fire,
What more could a weary old Santa desire?
So he puffed at his pipe and remarked to his wife,

"This amply makes up for my strenuous life!
From climbing down chimneys my legs fairly ache,
But it's well worth the while for the dear children's sake.
I'd bruise every bone in my body to see
The darlings' delight in a gift-laden tree!"
Just then came a sound like a telephone bell—
Though why they should have such a thing I can't tell—
St. Nick gave a snort and exclaimed in a rage,
"Bad luck to inventions of this modern age!"
He grabbed the receiver—his face wore a frown
As he roared in the mouthpiece, "I will not come down
To exchange toys like an up-to-date store,

Ring off, I'll not listen to anything more!"
Then he settled himself by the comforting blaze
And waxed reminiscent of halcyon days
When children were happy with simplest of toys:
A doll for the girls and a drum for the boys—
But again came that noisy disturber of peace
The telephone bell—would the sound never cease?
"Run and answer it, wife, all my patience has fled,
If they keep this thing up I shall wish I were dead!
I have worked night and day the best part of a year
To supply all the children, and what do I hear?
A boy who declares he received roller skates
When he wanted a gun, and a cross girl who states
That she asked for a new Victor talking machine
And I brought her a sled, so she thinks I am 'mean!'"
Poor St. Nicholas looked just the picture of woe,
He needed some auto-suggestion, you know,
To make him think things were all coming out right,
For he didn't get one wink of slumber that night!
The telephone wire kept sizzling-hot
By children disgusted with presents they'd got,

And when the bright sun showed its face in the sky
The Santa Claus family were ready to cry!
Just then something happened—a way of escape,
Though it came in the funniest possible shape—
A balloonist, sorely in need of a meal,
Descended for breakfast—it seemed quite ideal!
For the end of it was, he invited his host
Out to try the balloon, of whose speed he could boast.
St. Nick, who was nothing if not a good sport

Was delighted to go, and as quick as a thought
Climbed into the car for a flight in the air—
"No telephone bells can disturb me up there!
And, wife, if it suits me I'll count it no crime
To stay up till ready for next Christmastime!"
Thus saying, he sailed in the giant balloon,
And I fear that he will not return very soon.
Now, when you ask "Central" for Santa-Claus land
She'll say, "discontinued"—and you'll understand.

CHRISTMAS: ITS ORIGIN, CELEBRATION AND SIGNIFICANCE AS RELATED IN PROSE AND VERSE. EDITED BY ROBERT HAVEN SCHAUFFLER. NEW YORK: MOFFAT, YARD AND CO., 1913.

# "Tomorrow is Christmas Morning."

Gabrielle Stewart

Old Santa Claus woke from his long winter nap,
Put on his fur overcoat, muffler and cap,
Then ordered his reindeer and harnessed the sleigh;
"For I must be up and off and away,
Tomorrow is Christmas morning."
He blew on his horn for his Troopers so bold,
A myriad of them in numbers untold,
All mounted and booted in trapping so gay,
The Rocking Horse Troopers all leading the way,
For tomorrow is Christmas morning.
At the wave of his hand the Dollies all come,
Both little and big ones, they walk and they run,
Dressed up in fine muslins, silks, velvets and lace,
With merriment dancing on each pretty face,
For tomorrow is Christmas morning.
He went to the fields where sugarplums grow,
Millions of trees of them, row after row,
And bushels and bushels came tumbling adown,
Red ones and pink ones and chocolate brown,
For tomorrow is Christmas morning.
He pushes a button and trinkets galore

Come hustling and bustling right up to his door,
Horns, whistles and bells, drums, engines and toys,
Such beautiful gifts for our good girls and boys,
For tomorrow is Christmas morning.
And now he is off for his long Christmas ride,
To visit the children who live far and wide,
Wherever they live, and his sharp eyes can see
A stocking hung up or a bright Christmas tree,
For tomorrow is Christmas morning.

THE NEW YORK DAILY TRIBUNE, DECEMBER 24, 1901

# "The Christmas Dancing"

### Frank L. Stanton

The sparks were twinkling nightward like fireflies in
    the snow,
Far down the chilly road we saw the frosty windows
    glow
With the lights—the lights of Christmas—a bell in
    merry chime,
And "Hands round" in the quadrille, and the fiddler
    keeping time!
The cheery wind came whistling o'er the meadows and
    the plains,

And rattled us a welcome in the dancing window-
    panes;
And the rafters rang with music to the twinkling of
    our feet,
And the mistletoe was tempting, and the lips were red
    and sweet.
The fiddler called the "figures": "Now swing yer
    partners all!"
And "Ladies to the center!" went ringing down the
    hall

(The old time, sable fiddler, whose tunes could
    welcome win
From the jubilant plantations ere "the freedom days"
    came in!)
Ah, me, that Christmas dancing! Still—still I see the
    glow
Of cheeks and eyes entrancing, and lights across the
    snow!
How we met the morn with music, and whispered
    sweet farewells
To the ringing and the singing of the bells—the
    Christmas bells!
I hear the oak logs crackle—the fiddler's music seems
The sweetest that has ever made a ripple in my
    dreams!
The lights—the lights of Christmas, fringed with the
    frosty rime—
And the "Hands round" in the quadrille; and my heart
    is keeping time!

*THE SATURDAY EVENING POST*, DECEMBER 23, 1899

# Christmas in the News

# "President Harrison as 'Santa Claus'"

DAWSON, W.F. *CHRISTMAS:*
*ITS ORIGIN AND ASSOCIATIONS.*
LONDON: ELLIOT STOCK, 1902.

Writing from New York on December 22, 1891, a correspondent says: "President Harrison was seen by your correspondent at the White House yesterday, and was asked what he thought about Christmas and its religious and social influences. The President expressed himself willing to offer his opinions and said: 'Christmas is the most sacred religious festival of the year, and should be an occasion of general rejoicing throughout the land, from the humblest citizen to the highest official, who, for the time being, should forget or put behind him his cares and annoyances, and participate in the spirit of seasonable festivity. We intend to make it a happy day at the White House—all the members of my family, representing four generations, will gather around the big table in the State dining room to have an old-fashioned Christmas dinner. Besides Mrs. Harrison, there will be her father, Dr. Scott, Mr. and Mrs. M'Kee and their children, Mrs. Dimmick and Lieutenant and Mrs. Parker. I am an ardent believer in the duty we owe to ourselves at Christmas to make merry for children at Christmastime, and we shall have an old-fashioned Christmas tree for the grandchildren upstairs; and I shall be Santa Claus myself. If my influence goes for aught in this busy world let me hope that my example may be followed in every family in the land.'"

*from*

# "Christmas in America"

FROM *CHRISTMAS: ITS ORIGIN AND ASSOCIATIONS.*
LONDON: ELLIOT STOCK, 1902.

## W. F. Dawson

A curious feature of an American Christmas is the eggnog and free lunch, distributed at all the hotels and cafes. A week at least before the 25th, fanciful signs are suspended over the fountains of the bars (the hotel keepers are quite classic in their ideas) announcing superb lunches with eggnogs on Christmas Day. This invitation is sure to meet with a large response from the amateur epicures about town, who, ever on the qui vive for a banquet gratis, flock to the festive standard, since it has never been found a difficult matter to give things away, from the time corrupt Romans gastronomed in Phoenicia up to the present hour. A splendid hall in one of the principal hotels, at this moment, occurs to us. A table, the length of the apartment, is spread and furnished with twenty made dishes peculiar to the Christmas cuisine. There are *chorodens* and fricassees, ragouts, and *calipee*, of rapturous delicacy. Each dish is labeled, and attended by a black servant, who serves its contents on very small, white gilt-edged plates. At the head of the table a vast bowl ornamented with indescribable Chinese figures, contains the egg-nog—a palatable compound of milk, eggs, brandy, and spices, nankeenish in colour, with froth enough on its surface to generate any number of Venuses, if the old Peloponnesian anecdote is worth remembering at all. Over the egg nog mine host usually officiates, all smiles and benignity, pouring the rich draught with miraculous dexterity into cut-glass goblets, and passing it to the surrounding guests with profuse hand. On this occasion the long range of fancy drinks are forgotten. Sherry-cobblers, mint-juleps, gin-slings, and punches, are set aside in order that the sway of the Christmas draught may be supreme. Free lunches are extremely common in the United States, what are called "eleven o'clock snacks" especially; but the accompaniment of egg nog belongs unequivocally to the end of the year.

The presentation of "boxes" and *souvenirs* is the same in America as in England, the token of remembrance having an inseparable alliance with the same period. Everybody expects to give and receive. A month before the event the fancy stores are crowded all day long with old and young in search of suitable *souvenirs*, and every object is purchased, from costliest gems to the tawdriest *babiole* that may get into the market. If the weather should be fine, the principal streets are thronged with ladies shopping in sleighs; and hither and thither sleds shoot by, laden with parcels of painted toys, instruments of mock music and septuagenarian dread, from a penny trumpet to a sheepskin drum.

Christmas seems to be a popular period among the young folk for being mated, and a surprising number approach the altar this morning. Whether it is that orange-flowers and bridal gifts are admirably adapted to the time, or that a longer lease of happiness is ensured from the joyous character of the occasion, we are not sufficiently learned in hymnal lore to announce. The Christmas week, however, is a merry one for the honeymoon, as little is thought of but mirth and gaiety until the dawning New Year soberly suggests that we should put aside our masquerade manners.

In drawing room amusements society has a wealth of pleasing indoor pastimes. We remember the sententious Question reunions, the hilarious Surprise parties, Fairy-Bowl, and Hunt-the-Slipper. We can never forget the vagabond Calathumpians, who employ in their bands everything inharmonious, from a fire-shovel to a stewpan, causing more din than the demons down under the sea ever dreamed of.

What, then, between the sleigh rides, the bell melodies, old Santa Claus and his fictions, the eggnog and lunches, the weddings, and the willingness to be entertained, the Americans find no difficulty in enjoying Christmas Day. Old forms and new notions come in for a share of observances, and the young country, in a glow of good humor, with one voice exclaims, "Le bon temps vienara."

# "Gifts Crowd Wilsons"

FROM *THE WASHINGTON POST*, DECEMBER 24, 1916

## WHITE HOUSE CHRISTMAS GAIETY ENHANCED BY A BIG TREE.

### TURKEYS FOR 125 EMPLOYEES

Little Misses McAdoo and Cothran the Only Children Who Will Participate This Year—Home Celebrations Planned—President to Rest This Week—Appointments Few

Christmas gifts poured through the doors of the White House yesterday, ready for the celebration of the home holiday tomorrow. These presents from near and far are for the most part for the president or Mrs. Wilson, but there are included a considerable number for members of the family.

The president's immediate relatives have carefully sequestered their personal gifts for each other in numerous nooks and corners of the executive mansions in anticipation of the general exchange of remembrances which will be staged in the upper corridors of the White House just after breakfast tomorrow.

## "Center of the Festivity"

Yesterday the Christmas tree, which will form the central decoration of the festivity, was put in place and the afternoon was devoted to its decoration with pretty things and a generous chain of electric bulbs, which will shed their light over the scene.

Only two of the children of President Wilson's immediate family will participate in this year's reunion. They are little Miss Josephine Cothran, the president's grandniece, and his granddaughter, little Miss McAdoo, aged 2. The two children of Mr. and Mrs. Francis Bowed Sayre were left behind in their home at Williamstown, Mass., when their parents came to Washington for the Christmas weekend.

## "Joy for Married Employees"

Joy was conveyed yesterday to all the married employees of the White House, high and low, when 125 fine fat turkeys were distributed with the president's compliments and best wishes for a merry Christmas dinner. The secretarial and clerical staff, the policemen, who keep watch over the personal safety of Mr. Wilson, were all remembered.

President Wilson's plans for next week provide him with ample opportunity for rest and relaxation. His official appointments have been confined to a very few for Wednesday and Thursday. On Tuesday evening at 8:45 Mr. Wilson will open the Humboldt park Christmas celebration in Chicago by pressing an electric button in the White House.

*from*

# "Merry Christmas in the Tenements"

FROM *THE BOOK OF CHRISTMAS*. WITH AN INTRODUCTION BY
HAMILTON MABIE. NEW YORK: MACMILLAN, 1909.

## Jacob Riis

The lights of the Bowery glow like a myriad twinkling stars upon the ceaseless flood of humanity that surges ever through the great highway of the homeless. They shine upon long rows of lodging houses, in which hundreds of young men, cast help-less upon the reef of the strange city, are learning their first lessons of utter loneliness; for what desolation is there like that of the careless crowd when all the world rejoices? They shine upon the tempter setting his snares there, and upon the mis-sionary and the Salvation Army lass, disputing his catch with him; upon the police detective going his rounds with coldly ob-servant eye intent upon the outcome of the contest; upon the wreck that is past hope, and upon the youth pausing on the verge of the pit in which the other has long ceased to struggle. Sights and sounds of Christmas there are in plenty in the Bow-ery.

Balsam and hemlock and fir stand in groves along the bust thoroughfare, and garlands of green embower mission and dive impartially. Once a year the old street recalls its youth with an effort. It is true that it is largely a commercial effort; that the evergreen, with an instinct that is not of its native hills, haunt saloon corners by preference; but the smell of the pine woods is in the air, and—Christmas is not too critical—one is grateful for the effort. It varies with the opportunity. At Beefsteak John's it is content with artistically embalming crullers and mince pies in green cabbage under the window lamp. Over yonder, where the milepost of the old land still stands—in its unhonored old age become the vehicle of publishing the latest "sure cure" to the world—a florist, whose undenominational zeal for the holiday and trade outstrips alike distinction of creed and property, has transformed the sidewalk and the ugly railroad structure into a veritable bower, spanning it with a canopy of green, under which dwell with him, in neighborly goodwill, the Young Men's Christian Association and the Jewish tailor next door....

Down at the foot of the Bowery is the "panhandlers' beat," where the saloons elbow one another at every step, crowding out all other business than that of keeping lodgers to support them. Within call of it across the square, stands a church which, in the memory of men yet living, was built to shelter the fashionable Baptist audiences of a day when Madison Square was out in the fields, and Harlem had a foreign sound. The fashionable audiences are gone long since. Today the church, fallen into premature decay, but still handsome in its strong and noble lines, stands as a missionary outpost in the land of the enemy, its builders would have said, doing a greater work than they planned. Tonight is the Christmas festival of its Sunday school for the English-speaking, and the pews are filled. The banners of United Italy, of modern Greece, of France and Germany and England, hang side by side with the Chinese dragon and the starry flag-signs of the cosmopolitan character of the congregation. Greek and Roman Catholics, Jews and joss-stick worshipers, go there; few Protestants, and no Baptists. It is easy to pick out the children in their seats by nationality, and as easy to read the story of poverty and suffering that stands written in more than one mother's haggard face, now beaming with pleasure at the little ones' glee. A gayly decorated Christmas tree has taken the place of the pulpit. At its foot is stacked a mountain of bundles, Santa Claus's gifts to the school. A self-conscious young man with soap-locks has just been allowed to retire, amid tumultuous applause, after blowing "Nearer My God, to Thee" on his horn until his cheeks swelled almost to bursting: a trumpet overtakes the Fourth Ward by storm. A class of little girls is climbing upon the platform. Each wears a capital letter on her breast, and together they spell its lesson. There is momentary consternation: one is missing. As the discovery is made, a child pushes past the doorkeeper, hot and breathless. "I am in 'Boundless Love,'" she says, and makes for the platform, where her arrival restores confidence and the language.

In the audience the befrocked visitor from uptown sits cheek by jowl with the pigtailed Chinese man and the dark-browed Italian. Up in the gallery, farthest from the preacher's desk and the tree, sits a Jewish mother with three boys, almost in rags. A dingy and threadbare shawl partly hides her poor calico wrap and patched apron. The woman shrinks in the pew, fearful of being seen; her boys stand upon the benches, and applaud with the rest. She endeavors vainly to restrain them. "Tick, tick!" goes the old clock over the door through which wealth and fashion went out long ago and poverty came in....

# "Buying the Christmas Gobbler"

FROM *THE NEW YORK TRIBUNE*, DECEMBER 25, 1898

## Sights and Scenes in Washington Market Before the Crowd Went Home

In Washington Market last evening you could hear the "barkers" barking for blocks away, and it almost seemed as though the people in the elevated trains would catch disjointed sentences about "corn-fed spring turkeys" and "fine Christmas gobblers." And as for price—well, after 10 o'clock when the basket-carriers and the bargain-hunting women arrived from Hoboken and most anywhere else, the prices were of no importance at all. It will not be the fault of the Washington Market philanthropists if anyone in the metropolis hungers for turkey on Christmas Day '98.

"How is the turkey trade this season?" asked a *Tribune* reporter of a dealer who is declared to have few rivals in the market as an authority on turkeys.

"The supply this year has been enormous," was the answer. "The warm and muggy weather for the last few days has been bad for us. It has hurried the supply forward and cheapened it.

All these turkeys you see about the market and around the city come from the west—Indiana, Iowa, Illinois and Wisconsin. They run in weight from six to twenty pounds, but, of course, these birds, which cost from 10 to 16 cents a pound, are not the choicest turkeys. In fact, even the best of the western birds are put right into cold storage."

"How about the aggregate amount of Christmas turkey used in New York?" queried the reporter. "Would it be a hundred thousand pounds?" he asked. "Of course, that is a good deal of turkey," the reporter added apologetically.

"More likely, one hundred thousand tons, young man."

"Of turkey?"

"Of turkey. Of course, that is high, but not less than ten million pounds of turkey will be used in New York for the holiday season, and to that add a quarter as much chicken and another quarter of duck.

"The heaviest turkey I ever saw weighed forty-five pounds," continued the authority. "The biggest in the market this year weighed thirty-eight pounds. They seldom exceed that. This whole turkey business has really grown up to its present enormous proportions in the last twenty years. Why, back in '76 and '78 we paid 20 to 25 cents a pound wholesale for turkeys. The supply was limited and the demand also, but about this time on Christmas Eve the supply would run low and the price go up. We'd give up charging by the pound, and it was turkeys at $6 and $8 apiece, and people scrambling for the last one. In those days turkeys were luxuries. Now they are cheap enough for everybody."

Outside the market, where Vesey St.'s uneven pavement struggles down to the riverfront, the "barkers" were unloading unlimited turkeys on the public. Out there nobody thought about rice-fed Marylanders with black legs. It was just a question of turkey. At one stand a laborer was bargaining for a good-sized bird.

"Twelve pounds," said the dealer. "$1.68."

The man hesitated. "Lord! An' its ivery cint I've got to me name," he said.

In a jiffy the turkey was in a brown paper bag with legs protruding and laid on the customer's arm.

"Take yer bird, and here's a nickel to get home with," said the dealer as he gathered in the money.

"How much is chickens?" asked a small, thin woman.

"Twenty-eight cents, ma'am."

"Give yer twenty-five."

A flourish of the meat-ax, the head and legs flew in different directions, and before the woman could hedge, the decapitated and legless chicken was in her hand.

"She'll come again," said the market man, to the reporter, "they like to be pushed. You can't pick them wimmin up too quick."

"How about geese?" asked an old woman with a red shawl and a market basket.

"Ten a pound, ma'am."

He threw a goose on the scales. The customer hesitated. "You want the head I suppose?" he queried, and in a second a goose with dangling head was bundled into brown paper and shoved into the basket.

"See here," said a red-headed little man. "I've come down here Christmas Eve to give you a piece of my mind about that turkey you sold me for Thanksgiving. You're a fraud. I want to expose you. I went to carve that turkey and she wouldn't carve. Finally I got off the two legs, and my wife and I each tackled one, and when we got through, sir, with them two drumsticks, we'd each done a day's work, and we went and laid down. After that, the hired girl tackled that turkey to make hash of it, and she broke the chopper and cut her hand so she's in a hospital. You're a fraud and I'm here to tell about it."

The crow of "barkers" and bargain-hunters pushed the little man along, still explaining. And then the market man had his inning. He took the reporter by the sleeve and winked confidentially.

"Nice man," he said. "He's been a customer of ours going on fourteen years. He's only got one failing. Did you notice how red his face was? No? Well, that's it. Every Christmas Eve for fourteen years he's had a 'jag.' You heard what he said? Well, that's all jag. Too bad, ain't it? Nice man."

Then, with a rapid change of voice, he went on: "Step right up, gents, and get yer Christmas turkeys. Finest corn-fed gobblers. Choicest thing in the market. Only twelve cents a pound. Here you are, finest Christmas turkeys, just waitin' to be eat."

And at 11:15 o'clock the procession of brown-papered parcels with turkey legs protruding, was still moving north and south and east and over the river to the dark regions of New Jersey on the west.

# "Santa Claus Arrested"

FROM *THE BROOKLYN DAILY EAGLE*, MONDAY, DECEMBER 23, 1901

## Had Pilfered Bread and Milk—Was Drunk and Had No Home

An unfeeling policeman arrested Santa Claus this morning. At least, the man arrested tried to make the cop believe that he was old St. Nick. But for the benefit of the good little boys and girls it can be stated right here that it was not the really truly Santa Claus at all, but only a make-believe and evidently a bad one at that.

Officer Donlon of the Grand Avenue station saw a young man, who afterward admitted his name was John Jones, 20 years old, with no home, at the corner of Franklin and Atlantic Avenues. The man had a big bag over his back.

"Hi, there! Who are you?" asked the officer.

"Santa Claus," the man replied.

"What'cher got in the bag?"

"Presents for the poor kids."

"Let's see," said the cop, and, after delving into the bag, he brought out sixteen bottles of milk and eighteen loaves of bread. The milk was the property of William E. Rogers of 86 Butler Street, and was said to have been stolen from Von Glahn's store at Franklin Avenue and Bergen Street. Richter Brothers of

Classon Avenue and Dean Street claimed the bread, but didn't know where it was stolen from.

Jones told the magistrate this morning that he was drunk and was held for the Court of Special Sessions.

# "Turkeys for U.S. Army in France Are Too Late for Christmas; Ship with Cranberries Is Turned Back"

FROM *THE WASHINGTON POST*, DECEMBER 21, 1917

The great bulk of the American expeditionary force will not get its expected Christmas dinner. A submarine attack forced the ship which was carrying cranberries to turn back, and through some unknown circumstances two ships which were carrying the supplies of turkey left the United States so late that it was impossible for them to arrive in France in time.

The turkeys which already have arrived in the army zone were left over from Thanksgiving, as was the mince meat which has been received. This supply, however, will go an extremely short way.

## "Looking for a Substitute"

The quartermaster's corps is now busy trying to secure a substitute for the anticipated Christmas provender on this side of the Atlantic, but the army is disappointed, for turkey at Christmas has been looked forward to by virtually every member of the command. The quartermaster had made careful preparations, but his calculations went wrong, as today's announcement shows.

When the news became known among the forces there were loud cries of distress from many quarters and envious eyes were cast at the roaming French poultry. From the general outlook now it appears that the principal dish of the day will be "monkey turkey," which appears on the commissary list as ordinary canned corned beef.

Over one cook shack in the zone there has been pinned a striking picture of a gobbler, underneath which is written: "Take a good look! This is the only turkey in France, and I got it!"

# "Americans and British to Enjoy Christmas Together."

FROM *THE WASHINGTON POST*, DECEMBER 22, 1917

For the first time in history, British Tommies and American troops will celebrate Christmas together.

Arrangements were being completed today for a whole series of mutual holiday "shindigs" and "blow-outs"—circumstances permitting.

The Americans are widely scattered, making gatherings difficult and in some cases impossible—but some sort of a celebration is to be held wherever they have a chance to meet.

British fighting men, like the Americans, have their own gifts from home—gifts delivered even to dugouts and to their temporary shell-hole homes on the very first line.

Incidentally, a canvass of the Tommies by their commanding officers to find out just what sort of things they wanted for this Christmas spread, has developed some freakish appetites.

One captain asked his men whether they wanted turkey or pork and beans—the latter piping hot, with strips of bacon browned on the top. The pork and beans won hands down in the subsequent vote.

There will be no fraternizing on the British Front. That much is certain. Christmas Day in the trenches will be just like any other war day—depending on developments.

Today all the front was decorated in a mantle of snow a foot deep.

CHRISTMAS SUPPLEMENT
TO THE
ILLUSTRATED LONDON NEWS
DEC. 16
1871

# Christmas Past

# "New Year Calls In Old New York"

FROM *CURIOSITIES OF POPULAR CUSTOMS*, FROM
*THE BOOK OF CHRISTMAS*. WITH AN INTRODUCTION BY
HAMILTON MABIE. NEW YORK: MACMILLAN, 1909.

## W. S. Walsh

From old Dutch times to the middle of the nineteenth century, New Year's Day in New York was devoted to an universal interchange of visits. Old friendships were renewed, family differences settled, a hearty welcome extended ever to strangers of presentable appearance.

This following is an entry in Tyrone Power's—the actor's—diary for January 1, 1834: "On this day from an early hour every door in New York is open and all the good things possessed by the inmates paraded in lavish profusion. Every sort of vehicle is put in requisition. At an early hour a gentleman of whom I had a slight knowledge entered my room, accompanied by an elderly person I had never before seen and who, on being named, excused himself for adopting such a frank mode of making my acquaintance, which he was pleased to add he much desired, and at once requested me to fall in with the custom of the day, whose privilege he had thus availed himself of, and accompany him on a visit to his family.

"I was the last man on earth likely to decline an offer made in such a spirit; so entering his carriage which was waiting, we drove to his house on Broadway, where, after being presented to a very amiable lady, his wife, and a pretty gentle-looking girl, his daughter, I partook of a sumptuous luncheon, drank a glass of champagne, and on the arrival of other visitors, made my bow, well pleased with my visit.

"My host now begged me to make a few calls with him, explaining, as we drove along, the strict observances paid to this day throughout the State, and tracing the excellent custom to the early Dutch colonists. I paid several calls in company with my new friend, and at each place met a hearty welcome, when my companion suggested that I might have some compliments to make on my own account, and so leaving me, begged me to consider his carriage perfectly at my disposal. I left a card or two and made a couple of hurried visits, then returned to my hotel to think over the many beneficial effects likely to grow out of such a charitable custom, which makes even the stranger sensible of the benevolent influence of this kindly day, and wish for its continued observance."

At the period of which Power speaks there were great feasts spread in many houses and the traditions of tremendous Dutch eating and drinking were faithfully observed. Special houses were noted for particular forms of entertainment. At one it was eggnog, at another rum punch; at this one, pickled oysters, at that, boned turkey, or marvelous chocolate, or perfect mocha coffee; or, for the select cognoscenti a drop of old Madeira as delicate in flavor as the texture of the glass from which it was sipped. At all houses there were New Year's cakes, in the form of Egyptian monuments, and in later and more degenerate days, relays of champagne bottles appeared—the coming in of the lower empire.

Then followed the gradual breaking down of all lines of conventionality into a wild and unseemly riot of visits; New Year's Day took on a character of a rabid and untamed race against time. A procession, each of whose component parts was made up of two or three young men in an open carriage, with a pair of steaming horses and a driver more or less under the influences of the hilarity of the day, would rattle from one house to another all day long. The visitors would jump out of the carriage, rush into the house and reappear in a miraculously short space of time. The ceremony of calling was a burlesque. There was a noisy, hilarious greeting, a glass of wine was swallowed hurriedly, everybody shook hands all around, and the callers dashed out, rushed into the carriage, and were driven hurriedly to the next house.

A reaction naturally set in which ended in the almost complete disuse of the custom of New Year's calls.

# "Complicating Christmas"

FROM *THE LADIES' HOME JOURNAL*, DECEMBER 1899

There must be some radical and growing departure from the right and best way of celebrating Christmas when each recurring year we hear a larger number of men saying, "Well, I'll be truly thankful when this Christmas business is over." And they are led to this remark generally by seeing their wives, mothers, sisters or daughters reach Christmas Day utterly tired out, with the prospect of a siege of illness as soon as Christmas is over. And it must be confessed that this state of affairs exists in thousands of homes. Women themselves frequently acknowledge their satisfaction when the day is over. Now, there is always something wrong when we make a burden of our pleasures. And if one of our sources of pleasure in the calendar's greatest gala day is derived from a feeling of thankfulness that it is over, there is something askew either in the way we prepare for, or spend, the day.

The work of celebrating Christmas falls, for the main part, on women. Men think that they do their share if they provide the money for the Christmas purchases, and sparingly assist in the selection of an occasional present. And I suppose it is just as well that the buying of Christmas presents is not by custom delegated to men. For of all spectacles, a man deep in the problem of selecting a Christmas gift, especially one for a woman, is always the most interesting imaginable. One way of simplifying Christmas might be to let me buy all the presents. But I fear that if this were the case, the number of Christmas presents and Christmas merchants would soon be materially decreased. So after all, these duties have been pretty wisely placed in the hands best adapted to handle them. Yet the growing number of women who each year tire themselves out preparing for Christmas, and reach the day itself unfit to enjoy it properly, seems to indicate that sooner or later, if we go on, we shall reach the other extreme and abuse Christmas by overdoing its celebration. And if we look into the matter, we may find that we are complicating Christmas a bit and making it exactly the reverse of what the day really stands for.

# "Christmas Past and Present"

FROM *HARPER'S BAZAAR*, DECEMBER 31, 1881

"A Merry Christmas and a Happy New Year." Shall we ever grow tired of the kindly greeting? Our finest friend has no finer salutation, and the market man in his bower of paper roses, the grocery boy stamping stiffened feet at the area door, the cook flushed with responsibility over the heaped-up tables of her kitchen, the little crossing sweep blowing blue fingers of desire, pronounce the cheerful benediction as with no ultimate thought of gain. Nay, before the day deigns, has not the sound thereof roused us reluctantly from exhausted slumbers, as in the chill December darkness, the tittering, whispering, rapturous children tiptoe about to feel the bulging stockings it is yet too early to see? Yea, even for days and days before this top and crown of days, have not all the newspapers been exclaiming in the very fattest and blackest of capital letters that every shop in the city has more beautiful, more various, more abundant, and more preposterously cheap holiday presents than every other? And have not these glorified streets, these enchanted marts, these dazzling wares, these hurrying, smiling, eager crowds, been crying out over and over again, "Wish you a Merry Christmas and a Happy New Year"?

No, plainly, Christmas is a fashion that will never go out. And yet it is a fashion that has greatly changed within the memory of middle age. The Puritans left it religiously behind them when they packed up their carefully assorted traditions for transportation. No profane wassail, or Druidical mistletoe, or pagan custom of gift-giving, or heathenish Yule, encumbered them. And if perchance the scholarly Vane sent them an early copy of the poems of Mr. John Milton to his well-remembered friends in the new settlements of Massachusetts Bay, we may be sure that the "Ode to the Morning of Christ's Nativity" was very seldom read. In New England, therefore, gentle Christmas went long unrecognized, and it is only the present generation which has really done it fit honor, with music, and rejoicing, and incense of the fresh woods in breath of hemlock and mosses and pine.

Wherever the Establishment took root, however, or wherever the Roman Catholic element was strong, in the great German stream flowed into the New World reservoirs, there the Christmas feeling came also. In New York, and Virginia, and the South, was vast hospitality of eating and drinking, some exchange of gifts, and a limited churchgoing. Yet, here again it is only this generation which sees Christmas as the universal holiday, the general festival taken out of the pale of Catholic or Episcopal possession, and made the property of all sects, as of all ranks and no ranks.

But in South and North alike, Christmas past was a narrow and self-seeking spirit as compared with Christmas present.

Christmas past, roused perhaps by the gentle praise of Irving, made family feasts, rejoiced the children of the households with gifts, taught the elders to look back and sigh for the bounteous merry-making of the olden time. But Christmas present, of which Dickens was the great apostle, and for whose coming he made the way straight, is the spirit of unselfish kindness. Every year the churches are more beautiful, but the gorgeous fruitage of the trees that grow in their vestries is for the children who would have no Christmas else. Every year the shops are more splendid, and wealth and love give costlier gifts to their own, but every year, also, more men and women save something from the sum to be spent on kin and friend for those who can claim only the human tie for remembrance. Every year more ragged schoolchildren, and newsboys, and bootblacks, and sufferers in hospitals, and patient folk in almshouses, and long-hopeless inmates of asylums and prisons, are remembered in kindness. Every year more hard-worked men and women get the brief holiday for their homely uses. Every year there is more friendliness in the air.

So, it seems that the true Christmas, like the kingdom of heaven, of which, indeed, it is a part, is within us. It is the hour of charitable thoughts and active service. It is our season of vision, when eyes are anointed to see how easy it is to bestow it. To most of us, indeed, an underlying sadness must deepen a little by contrast with the external joy. We think of those past Christmases of our youth, each of which in turn was to have seen us great, or rich, or famous, or noble, or happy, with the fulfillment of some desire which was never to be satisfied. We think of the friends whose greeting was the best of Christmas to us, and whose voices we shall no more hear. Filling the children's stockings, we long unutterably for the child who was to grow up only in the life to come. But these aspirations, ambitious, loves are not dead. Let us not try to forget, but give all a place at our Christmas fire, rich, very rich, in what we have, richer in what we fancy we have lost.

# "My Childish Faith in Santa Claus Was Rewarded"

FROM *THE LADIES' HOME JOURNAL*, DECEMBER 1901

Once, long ago when I was a little girl, I was with my father in a camp in the mines of Colorado. Six months of the year we were snowed in. There was no getting any distance from the camp except on snowshoes. Christmas Eve came, and with my heart all in a flutter, I went to bed wondering what Santa Claus would put into my stocking.

"He will surely come, won't he, Father?" I asked.

"Oh yes, he will come, but I doubt if he can carry much. We can't get out, but I think his reindeer will manage to get in."

"But how can he get the doll down the chimney if the fire is going?"

I had been longing for a doll with eyes and nose—not a wooden doll cut out of a pipe stick like the only one I possessed.

I grew so distressed over the fire that my father agreed to take out a window pane, assuring me that Santa Claus could get through very small places. However, I could not sleep for fear he would try the chimney and not knowing about the window would grow discouraged and go away. So one of the miners got a great plank and wrote on it in charcoal in big letters "Go Through the Window," and put it on top of the shanty. Then after being told again and again that Santa Claus could read all languages I went to sleep. Next morning I fairly fell out of bed and actually rolled toward my stocking in my intense anxiety to see if there were anything in it.

Yes, there was the doll. Such a beauty. Holding it up to the light of the window I saw the eyes and nose and red cheeks; then, and no one knows why, I burst into tears and fairly bellowed, dancing about the room, crazy-fashion, until I ran into my father's arms.

There were sixteen miners witness to my joy, and not a dry eye was there in the room when I had finished my capers.

The doll was made entirely out of white potatoes. One of the miners who knew something about carving concocted the plan, and with some wire and sticks and ink and paint, and the help of others who could sew and make clothes out of flour sacks and salt bags, this Christmas dolly grew into a great beauty.

"It pays a million times over," said one old-timer as he patted me on the head and remarked that he was glad Santa Claus came my way.

I did not understand until long afterward that there was a scarcity of provisions in camp, and the snowstorms were increasing. Or that Father had forbidden the cutting up of the potatoes to make me a plaything. But the men held a council on the question, and Father was overruled. Potatoes at that time were two hundred dollars a sack.

# "A Merry Christmas to You"

FROM *CHRISTMAS: ITS ORIGIN, CELEBRATION AND SIGNIFICANCE AS RELATED IN PROSE AND VERSE*. EDITED BY ROBERT HAVEN SCHAUFFLER. NEW YORK: MOFFAT, YARD AND CO., 1913.

Theodore Ledyard Cuylers

My own boyhood was spent in a delightful home on one of the most beautiful farms in Western New York—an experience that any city-bred boy might envy. We had no religious festivals except Thanksgiving Day and Christmas, and the latter was especially welcome, not only on account of the good fare but its good gifts. Christmas was sacred to Santa Claus, the patron saint of good boys and girls. We counted the days until its arrival. If the night before the longed-for festival was one of eager expectation in all our houses, it was a sad time in all barnyards and turkey coops and chicken roosts; for the slaughter was terrible, and the cry of the feathered tribes was like "the mourning of Hadadrimmon." As to our experiences within doors, they are portrayed in Dr. Clement C. Moore's immortal lines, "The Night Before Christmas," which is probably the most popular poem for children ever penned in America. As the visits of Santa Claus in the night could only be through the chimney, we hung our stockings where they would be in full sight. Three score and ten years ago such modern contrivances as steam pipes, and those unpoetical holes in the floor called "hot-air registers," were as entirely unknown in our rural regions as gas-burners or telephones. We had a genuine fireplace in our kitchen, big enough to contain an enormous backlog, and broad enough for eight or ten people to form "a circle wide" before it and enjoy the genial warmth.

The last process before going to bed was to suspend our stockings in the chimney jambs; and then we dreamed of Santa Claus, or if we awoke in the night, we listened for the jingling of his sleigh bells. At the peep of day we were aroused by the voice of my good grandfather, who planted himself in the stairway and shouted in a stentorian tone, "I wish you all a Merry Christmas!" The contest was as to who should give the salutation first, and the old gentleman determined to get the start of us by sounding his greeting to the family before we were out of our rooms. Then came a race for the chimney corner; all the stockings came down quicker than they had gone up. What could not be contained in them was disposed upon the mantel-piece, or elsewhere. I remember that I once received an autograph letter from Santa Claus, full of good counsels; and our dear old cook told me that she awoke in the night and, peeping into the kitchen, actually saw the veritable old visitor light a candle and sit down at the tale and write it! I believed it all as implicitly as I believed the Ten Commandments, or the story of David and Goliath. Happy days of childish credulity, when fact and fiction were swallowed alike without a misgiving! During my long life I have seen many a daydream and many an air-castle go the way of Santa Claus and the wonderful "Lamp of Aladdin."

In after years, when I became a parent, my beloved wife and I, determined to make the Christmastide one of the golden times of the twelve months. In midwinter, when all outside vegetation was bleak and bare, the Christmas tree in our parlor bloomed in many-colored beauty and bounty. When the tiny candles were all lighted the children and our domestics gathered round it and one of the youngsters rehearsed some pretty juvenile effusion; as "they that had found great spoil." After the happy harvesting of the magic tree in my own home, it was my custom to spend the afternoon or evening in some mission school and to watch the sparkling eyes of several hundreds of children while a huge Christmas tree shed down its bounties. Fifty years ago, when the degradation and miseries of the "Five-Points" were first invaded by pioneer philanthropy, it was a thrilling sight to behold the denizens of the slums and their children as they flocked into Mr. Pease's new "House of Industry" and the "Brewery Mission" building. The angelic host over the hills of Bethlehem did not make a more welcome revelation to them "who had sat in darkness and the shadow of death." In these days the squalid regions of our great cities are being explored and improved by various methods of systematic beneficence. "Christian Settlements" are established; bureaus of charity are formed and associations for the relief of the poor are organized. A noble work; but, after all, the most effective "bureau" is one that, in a waterproof and a stout pair of shoes, sallies off on a

wintry night to some abode of poverty with not only supplies
for suffering bodies but kind words of sympathy for lonesome
hearts. A dollar from a warm hand with a warm word is worth
two dollars sent by mail or by a messenger boy. The secret of
power in doing good is *personal contact*. Our incarnate "Elder
Brother" went in person to the sick chamber. He anointed with
His own hand the eyes of the blind man and He touched the
loathsome leper into health. The portentous chasm between
wealth and poverty must be bridged by a span of personal kindness over which the footsteps must turn in only one direction.
The personal contact of self-sacrificing benevolence with darkness, filth and misery—that is the only remedy. Heart must
touch heart. Benevolence also cannot be confined to calendars.
Those good people will exhibit the most of the spirit of our
Blessed Master who practice Christmas-giving and cheerful,
unselfish and zealous Christmas-living through all the circling
year.

# "Christmas Croaking"

From *The Brooklyn Daily Eagle*, Sunday, December 22, 1889

C. R. C.

## The Festival of Forty Years Ago and That of Today:

### A Bachelor Brought Up in Brooklyn Cracks the Good Old Times Chestnut and Rails Against the Modern Merchant— Both Sides of the Question.

"Christmas is not what it used to be." So say all the old-timers, many of them with a regretful shake of the head, and some of them with the added remark that "It's impossible to tell what the world is coming to." Croakers are they, every one of them; men and women who are wedded to the past and who, being pessimists to a certain degree, like the Old Brooklynite, can see no good in the present. The same people will tell you that Sunday has lost the charm it possessed some fifty years ago, and that much of the sweetness of Saturday has been swept away by the march of modern ideas. If sufficiently provoked they would no doubt go so far as to claim that the plain Long Island egg of commerce has lost its toothsomeness, and that the pumpkin pie of '89 is not the delicacy they were accustomed to masticate in their youth.

It has always been so. When a man has passed middle life his capacity for enjoyment decreases rapidly, and it is not remarkable that he should retain a fondness for the ways and customs of his youth, when keen delight was possible, and the canker worm of disappointment had not appeared upon the scene. Still, the old fellows should be allowed to grumble. It is one of the few privileges accorded to age, and occasionally while listening to their railings against what is, one may glean valuable and interesting information concerning what has been.

"What was this old Christmas of yours by the memory of which you set so much store and of which you are always boasting?" asked the writer the other day of a well preserved bachelor of 65 or thereabouts, who has spent all his life in Brooklyn.

"What was it?" he echoed, his anger rising at the question. "I'll tell you what it was in this neighborhood, anyway, and when I get through I don't think you will be inclined to believe that it has been improved upon. Let me begin with the weather. I suppose you think the weather you have nowadays is everything it ought to be. It's English enough to suit the present generation, but it doesn't suit me. When I was a boy, and for many a year afterward, good cold bracing weather used to set on about the end of November and would last clear through to March. About Christmas we always looked for plenty of snow—snow which came to stay awhile—and it was not often that we were disappointed. You have seen that picture of old Brooklyn in which the streets were all shining white; well that was the way the town looked every winter when I was growing up.

"Plenty of sleighing? I should say there was. Wheels were laid aside almost entirely for a couple of months, and everywhere you could hear the merry jingling of the bells. About Christmas? Well, I was coming to that if you had only given me time. To begin with, Christmas Day was not as long when I was a boy as it is now. It appears to me the present Christmas sets in about December 10 and winds up on December 31. For this extension of the period I hold the modern storekeeper entirely responsible. The people would be content with the old-fashioned three or four days or week at the most, but the shop man won't let them. Just as soon as December sets in, these industrious chasers of the nimble sixpence open the campaign which is to result in profits sufficient to make up for any possible slackness in trade during the rest of the year. Their first step is to advertise, of course. If they neglected this precaution all else would avail them nothing. Of that I am well aware, old fogy as I am. They fill the papers with catchy statements concerning the beauty and cheapness of their stock, all of which has been bought at a bargain and is especially suited for Christmas presents. There are Christmas dining tables, Christmas beds, Christmas stoves, Christmas hats, Christmas bonnets, Christmas crockery, Christmas cloaks at $12.49, former price $18.23; Christmas whisky and cigars and I do not know what else— everything, I suppose. Following the first discharge of advertisements comes the shop window display, calculated to set people talking about the enterprising merchant who is so good as to provide amusement for the children for nothing. One gets up a group of red-cheeked ladies and gentlemen clad in furs of the latest style who are waiting in front of an impossible country mansion for the sleigh and four horses just turning the corner. The temptation to ticket the costly garments must be a terrible one, but to the credit of the managers of the show it must be said that they do not succumb to it. Then another puts on his little stage a skating party, each member wearing exactly the kind of clothes most suitable for the amusement. Another exhibits a dolls' fair, another, a family dinner, not forgetting to bring out the family plate and glass. I might go on forever enumerating the artifices employed by the energetic tradesmen to whoop up the festive season and incidentally to spur on the laggards who are slow to open their purses. It is a great Christmas we have nowadays, to be sure, but it is the Christmas of the storekeepers, not of the people. They have made the season what it is and will keep it so long as they can. They have begun to boom Eastertide, too, and now you have Easter presents and Easter everything else just the same as at Christmas. By and by there will be Thanksgiving vanity sets and Fourth of July slippers, all wool and a yard wide. Bah! This mercenary spirit makes me tired."

Seeing that the old gentleman was becoming excited and mixed in his metaphors, as it were, I ventured to suggest that it would be pleasanter to recall some of the memories of Christmas as it was before the dry-goods people secured it as a peg on which to hang their wares.

"Certainly, certainly," he went on. "I was coming to that if you had not interrupted me—you funny people want a man to do two things at once. Well, as I was about to remark when you broke the current of my thoughts, Christmas some thirty or forty years ago was not what it is now. It was not heralded three or four weeks in advance by the beating of mercantile drums and the blowing of bargain-counter trumpets and all that sort of thing, but was looked forward to quietly as a day to be spent with one's family or friends in an unostentatious and decorous manner. Church-going people made a point of going to church in the morning. The presents had been given and received previously. And let me tell you there was none of that promiscuous scattering of gifts which later custom has made almost imperative. Presents were exchanged among people who had regard for each other, but were not thrust on mere acquaintances, as they are now, simply because it is the fashion. A man of moderate means who moves in society at this day shudders at the approach of Christmas, and well he may. Pardon me, if I appear at times to look at the world through green glasses. I cannot help it, my young friend. But to resume. After church there was the family dinner, always taken early, and at which all the members who could manage it were present. Then in the afternoon there was sleighriding down the road for the young folks, and at night a quiet social time around the parlor fire. Places of amusement were not much frequented by staid and solid people on Christmas day. No, sir, it was observed in a semireligious way, which I am sorry to say seems to have gone out of fashion. We enjoyed ourselves, let me tell you that, but quietly and as became respectable citizens. There was none of that wholesale guzzling at public bars which is now a feature of the season, and none of that promiscuous treating which makes the morrow so unpleasant. There was social drinking, but it was never allowed to go beyond the limits of moderation. What do I propose to do next Christmas Day? Well, I shall go to church, as usual, dine with an old friend and then shut myself up in my room for the rest of the day, so that I may escape witnessing the revels which night will surely bring.

Part of the conversation I had with my bachelor and somewhat frostbitten friend, I repeated to another old gentleman, the father of a large family, as jolly at 70 as he was at 25, I have no doubt. He laughed heartily at the recital, and laying his forefinger snugly alongside his nose, said, "Your bachelor may be a very upright and truth-loving gentleman, but he seems as though he were determined to look at things crosswise, and I am sure in some particulars he is a 'little off,' as you young people say. Don't you go away with the impression that the Christmas Day of old was a day of melancholy and straight-laced interchange of courtesy. There was plenty of fun in Brooklyn about the end of December, forty years ago, long before the merchant princes began to get in their fine work. I am telling you this and I ought to know. Those who felt like going to church did so, and enjoyed themselves not the less heartily afterwards. We had no theaters of any account then but we did not die of ennui, brought on by the lack of them. A fine day, and it was nearly always fine in the time I speak of, brought out every sleigh in the city, and the scene 'down the road' was one to be remembered. Then there were the roadhouses—great institutions they were in those days, too, and well patronized. Why, I have seen scores of turnouts tied to the fences just because there was no room for them in the hotel yards, and if a man needed anything hot, as most of us did, he had to possess his soul in patience until he got it. *Eggnog* found much favor about Christmastide, and if my memory serves me right, it deserved it. Then the chop-houses in town, they were all in the heyday of prosperity then, did a glorious business on Christmas night. Most of them provided a dinner for their patrons, and after that there were a few hours, the like of which the present generation has no chance of enjoying. I doubt if young fellows nowadays could stand what we did. Maybe our heads were harder or maybe science had not been brought to bear on the ageing of what we called for. There was nothing wrong with the Christmas Day of young Brooklyn, nor can any complaint be found with the way it is observed in these years of our Lord. 'Times change and we change with them,' as the poet remarks, and 'The world do move.' What does it profit us old fellows to kick? Let us take the goods which the gods provide and enjoy them as best we are able."

# Christmas Presents

*from*

# "What Children Ask of Santa Claus"

THE LADIES' HOME JOURNAL, DECEMBER 1898

Patti Lyle Collins

Reproduced by Special Permission of Mr. D.B. Leibhardt, Superintendent of the Dead Letter Office

Every year during the month of December there arrive at the Dead Letter Office in Washington several thousand letters from children all over the country intended for their patron saint, Santa Claus.

Only once on record has a letter been sent after the holidays returning thanks, and though it sometimes happens that gifts are asked for Mamma and Papa, it is not usual. There is generally a decided stress upon "I want." Some children, boys generally, know what they want, and have no hesitation to ask for it in "stand and deliver" tone. Others put in the plea of having been very good children "ever since last Christmas Day."

One little girl wrote last year from Los Angeles bribing "dear old Santa Claus" with two pressed violets. She modestly did not mention them, but allowed the graceful tribute to speak for itself. Another asked for his picture. He is deluged with promises of good behavior for the next year in case he obligingly complies with all the requests made this year.

While many of the letters are unmistakably the work of childish brains and hands, occasionally the instructions are so explicit and unusual that one suspects old heads are using this means to get a hearing and assistance in some unexpected quarter—as, for instance, when sandwiched in between the request for dollies and candies there is given the information that "my father is a grower of tube roses and would like to get a contract from some rich gentleman for the next season."

Many of these childish epistles are addressed to Santa Claus, care of the large firms who deal in toys and Christmas goods. They all come under the head of "fictitious" matter, and are sent to the Dead Letter Office, where they are first cut open to see that they contain nothing of value, and are then destroyed. Among the recent ones was one that had by accident slipped into the mail in England and reached this country. It was addressed to "Mr. Santa Claus, Green Mountain, Vermont."

There seems to be no doubt as to the primary instincts of children, no matter what education and emancipation may develop, for the boys nearly always want soldier suits, steam engines, milk wagons, horses, and such things as indicate to them power and business pursuits; and the girls, first, last, and continuously ask for dolls, providing that the mother instinct dominates all else.

The eternal feminine is also manifest in the humble petition for "a tub, an iron, a washboard." It may herald the dawn of progress in a dark corner whence comes the request for a tooth-brush and a comb.

The letters given on this page were those which were turned over to the Dead Letter Office at Washington during the holiday season 1897-98.

Perhaps among the millions of letters written during the year there are none to whom the performance is such an unmixed joy as these little correspondents of Santa Claus.

*Mr. Santycaus*
   Dear Sir: Will you come to me and my little sister we like to play. Please send us dolls and everything nice and we will thank you if you will come. We will not be very afraid of you, if you do not look at us much. Be sure and come my little sister and I will look for you every day.
*Your little girls*
Come to

Santycaus
Lizzie, Croton on Hudson, N.Y.

*Dear Santa Claus:*
   I want a big doll. With blue eyes and pretty hair, and I want some candy please. I want a Christmas tree. And bring Papa and Mamma something, and please remem-

ber the poor little girls to, and bring the baby and George something and I am eight years old and I live on Market Street. Good By.

*From Helen Varll.*

*Dear Santa Claus:*

I would like to have a very large doll, and a machine and a doll's bed, and please bring a xmas tree, please have the doll in white clothes and I would like to have pillows and blankets and sheets.

Your little friend,

Elsie Mills
New York

*Dear Santa Claus:*

I wish to have a sleigh and a doll head with nice long white curles and a chair.

*Emma Martin*

Warrensburg, MO, Dec. 25, 1897

*Dear Santa:*

I will write you a letter to thank you for so many nice things you brought me I never had such a nice Christmas in my life. Mr. Wagner and Mr. Theodore was down here and we had a nice time we ate pop corn and candy and thought it was nice. I thought the Christmas tree was beautiful and the candles was so pretty when they was burning. Mr. Theodore and Mr. Wagner thought the

house was a fire and they ran down the road to get here.
After you left we saw a light under the door. I will close
now.

Good by.
*From Bessie Bliss*

December 24, 1897

*My Dear and Loving Santa Claus:*
    I would like you to bring me a few presents as I have
all your presents since last Christmas. I would like a
game of Nellie Bly as I am very fond of games and if you
aint got the game of Nellie Bly please bring me a game of
fishing pond as I would rather have a game of Nellie Bly.
And my dear Santa Claus please bring me a great big
dolls carriage and I would like a large blackboard.
And that is all I want this Christmas.
Yours truly,

Agnes Smith
Newton Centre

123

# "A Budget of Christmas Suggestions"

FROM *THE LADIES' HOME JOURNAL*, DECEMBER 1904

### Cora B. Bickford

## What a Farmer's Wife Did

A Bride who began her housekeeping on a farm found, when Christmas Day drew near, that it was impossible for her to go to town to buy gifts for some of her girlfriends who also were keeping house, so this is what she did:

When planting corn her husband planted pumpkins, too, and this particular season there were an unusually large stock of them on hand for her to use. She selected several of the best, cut them in halves, carefully removed all the seeds, placed in each hollow interior a plump, tender, dressed chicken, arranged potatoes and other vegetables around the chicken in quantity sufficient for the Christmas dinner, and finally put in a tumbler of currant jelly.

And how her girlfriends did enjoy those gifts!

# "The Art of Christmas Shopping"

FROM *HARPER'S BAZAAR*, DECEMBER 17, 1881

There is one period of the year when a wild spirit of excitement seems to seize the quiet every-day world. It is like a top which is set rolling, and begins by moving slowly at first, with a monotonous hum, then spins on faster and faster, until one can scarcely follow it in its maze. So it is with Christmas. At first no one intends making any presents for *this* year. No, not even a card shall be sent. Presently the gay shop windows attract attention. You must just look over the Christmas cards, and see what the new ones look like. Then you cannot help purchasing a few. The cards lead you to other investments, and before you know it you are the most eager of the Christmas shoppers.

Few practical rules would prevent much loss of time, and after-regret. First, know what you want; then, for whom you want it; lastly, how much money you can spend on it. Let this all be settled before beginning the important work, remembering to adapt your purchases first to your purse, next to your friends. If through the year past a friend has expressed a wish to possess any little article of luxury or comfort, bear it in mind, and let the receiving it at your hands be a Christmas surprise. Or if you have visited at houses where you have been made welcome, show your sense of the compliment by some fitting gift. For instance, if you have had cozy talks around an open fire, what a bright remembrance of such evenings would be a little fancy brass shovel and tongs, or some trifle suggestive of a warm fireside! Or if the table at which you have been a guest in hours gone by had been bountifully spread, and sweetened with smiles and lively conversation, it may recall some of those pleasant hours for the family you have visited to see afterward a silver pepper owl, a set of dainty mats, or a dozen Japanese butter plates sent as a souvenir by "one of the circle" at Christmas. If the friend or relative whom you intend to remember is keeping house, some article of household ornament is always acceptable. If boarding, or about to travel abroad, then something for personal wear or convenience is more suitable, such as a bag, a portable writing desk, or a *couvre-pied*.

Now to adapt all these several articles to the various requirements, tastes, and circumstances of your friends requires time and thought, and some knowledge of character and circumstances. Do not give a book to one who never reads, if it be ever so highly prized by yourself, or lace to one debarred from society.

There are some things, too, that are admirably fitted to Christmas, and others which it is not good taste, or rather, good feeling, to bestow at such a time. Do not let your friends suspect that your remembrance is actuated more by charity than regard, for their poverty is the last thing they wish to have obtruded upon their notice at Christmas. A young girl might be pleased with a lace pin or a shell comb, who would resent a pair of gloves or a bonnet as a reflection upon her appearance. Give such a one some luxury that she can not feel it right to afford for herself, reserving more useful donations for other occasions, so that your Christmas gifts may be viewed in the light of charming surprises, not humiliations.

Christmas is not the time for making expensive presents. Leave those for weddings and birthdays. The simpler the gift, the more suitable, the more Christmassy, will it be. We all remember the Eastern tale where the wreath of flowers culled at even shone, by some occult magic, the next morning in all the resplendent hues of precious stones and ablaze with diamonds. Even so your little sprigs of holly, your wreaths of evergreen, that look perhaps homely and commonplace the day before, can be converted by the weird charm of Christmastide to peerless offerings more worthy of acceptance than the most costly gifts at any other time.

Christmas is no time to remind your friends of their infirmities, even for their souls' good. Keep books of sermons and moral essays for more suitable occasions.

Do not present a person who, while advancing in years, is diligently and creditably trying to preserve intact the graces and charms of her earlier days, with *The Evening of Life*, or *Consolations for the Aged*; do not give a hopeless invalid a convenient traveling case, or one with failing eyesight a volume of tantalizing engravings. Those whose poor fingers are weary with mothers' work do not find gold thimbles or darning bags any alleviation of their daily toil. Give to such something bright and tasteful to remind them that life is not all drudgery, or they mere drudges.

In the list for Christmas shopping do not let the young and happy forget the aged and the unhappy. Such value extremely any little attentions, and treasure them up with heartfelt thankfulness little dreamed of by those who only have to wish to receive.

If you had a clear idea of what you want, and for whom you want it, the poor distracted shopgirls would have an easier time. As it is, too often they not only have to show goods, but also to select them to suit the ideas and tastes of perfect strangers, with whose means they are totally unacquainted. No sooner does such a shopper decide upon one article and put it aside than something else, totally different, meets her eye, and directly a change must be made, which in too many cases is sadly and unavailingly repented of at home. Pretty articles are tossed about and snatched off the counter by eager purchasers, who would stand a far better chance of selection, and be much more comfortable, if, instead of choosing Christmas Eve as the time for spending their little hoard so long cherished and set aside for the luxury of presents, they would go quietly out a week—yes, even a month—beforehand, with a clear idea of what they want, for whom they want each article, how much money they mean to pay on an average for each purchase, and perhaps one might add why they want it.

In remembering our friends, our gifts should be the spontaneous outpouring of our hearts, not the cold, dry, calculating result of a debtor and creditor ledger, whereby the claims of society and relationship are satisfied, and "naught beyond."

Another reason for being early in the field in Christmas shopping is that there is less danger of being robbed. When there is a rush and a crush, it is very hard to keep your wits about you, or your purse about you either. If the first go astray, the second is very apt to follow.

Then, again, the range of selection is much greater early than if you wait until the best is picked out and you have to put up with the remnants left by more fortunate shoppers. Even in a great city there is a choice, and many a one sees, some little time beforehand, "just what she wants" in china or books, and, secure of purchasing the coveted prize at any time, calls for it a day or two before Christmas, only to find that it is gone, and nothing else as desirable is to be found in a hurried search involving much waste of time and patience.

To those whose friends are many and dollars few, we would commend Christmas cards, which are always in good taste. They oftentimes accompany a gift, but they can speak very eloquently when they are sent by themselves. Devote some portion of your time and energies to the selection of fitting cards by which to express your good wishes. Do not gather them up in a handful, as if you were shuffling for a deal in whist, or so many for one dollar, and then leave the choice to the saleswoman, expecting her to supply brains as well as cards. Christmas cards are among the very few things which are lovely in spite of being cheap. Some are radiant with a religious halo; some recall summer's birds and flowers in the midst of winter's gloom; others are bright with winter's charm of frost and snow; all are expressive of some sentiment, varied to suit different tastes. Adapt those you send to the ideas and characters of those for whom they are intended. Diaries and calendars never come amiss to rich or poor, and as in general they command a set price, it cannot seem mean to give what is always the best of its kind, besides linking yourself in the remembrance of another in each passing day's record.

There are many exquisite little volumes in poetry and prose of a religious, contemplative nature, bound daintily to suit the season. These are lovely remembrances for those to whom the very word Christmas only brings sad memories, who cannot join in the festivities of the time, yet who might feel hurt if entirely passed by.

To those of slender means but large hearts we would also commend, in the selection of inexpensive gifts that are always acceptable, baskets and chinaware. Who can resist a basket! Who, in the country, can ever see the basket maker's wagon going by without an irresistible longing to rifle its contents, or in the city pass a basket maker's den without "just stopping in." Who ever had as many baskets as he or she wanted? And who ever had too many?

There are the scrap basket and the gardening basket and the flower-and-fruit basket, and the work basket and knitting basket, to say nothing of baby baskets, and little children's dear possessions in that way.

Many of these you can ornament yourself, and thus enhance their value, either with ribbons or crewelwork, or both together, and thus have a tasteful present at small cost. As to china, the theme is simply inexhaustible. There are all the quaint little majolica pitchers and Japanese teapots and cups and saucers and flower holders in all sorts of odd shapes and sizes. Did any woman ever express herself as satisfied with the amount of china she possessed? If you buy such an article yourself, you look lovingly at it, and think how pretty it would appear on your own buffet, or in your hanging cabinet, or filled with flowers on your dinner table, and you sigh. There is the real sacrifice to friendship. And it cost *only*—do not reveal the secret; that might kill the charm. Now you have selected it, and relinquished it too, for the sake of a Christmas offering, all the wealth of Aladdin's lamp could not redeem it. Its money value is sunk in its sentimental value. Indeed, may not this truly be said of all Christmas gifts?

The transforming genii have touched them with the wand of an enchanter. You paid that patient young man or that smiling girl so many shillings in money value for them, but once in your possession, henceforth they are priceless.

*from*

# "Concerning Christmas Gifts"

FROM *THE BROOKLYN DAILY EAGLE*, DECEMBER 23, 1900

## By Julian Croskey

There is only one way of making a man a present of cigars. You have got to ask him to dinner half a dozen times and try a different brand on him at each. When he stops talking, smokes to a finish, and says, "By gad, Jones, I have enjoyed that smoke," you may send him a hundred and he will remember you every Sunday for a year. Send him a box of cigars that a commission agent has sent you, and at the end of the year you will find yourself mysteriously boycotted by a wide circle of acquaintance. The man—and his name is legion—who keeps the box of cabbage weed his wife gave him and palms them off to his friends, deserves to be shot. Do anything else you like to a man, but never give him a bad cigar or bad whisky which politeness forbids him to throw away. I have reduced my circle of acquaintance by at least fifty percent for this offense—on their part.

As to cigarettes, it is both an easier and a harder question. To the young man, you are always safe in sending a box of expensive ones, with gilt mouthpieces or a gilt crest on the paper, whatever tobacco they are made of. He keeps them on a silver box on his table and feels glorious in saying, "Have a cigarette," and he can always buy Sweet Caporal for himself. But for the discriminating smoker you must use discrimination. Never give him a widely advertised brand, which is sold in ten-cent packages. They are all trash; the ten cents pays for the advertisement. Good Turkish or Egyptian cigarettes are a luxury to some men. And owing to their narcotic properties, a pleasant occasional medicine to others. But they make a confounded smell in a room. If I knew of a good Virginia cigarette I should go out of my way to advertise it; I don't. One of the best has a paper which always frays in the mouth; another never draws. A good cigarette should never require a holder. The virtue of a cigarette as a present resides in the box and ashtray. This is what I am going to send young Tarveytop. He is a steady-going, industrious youth and a little clique of goody-goody counter jumpers visit him each Sunday. They bring their own cigarettes; but Tarvey has a job brushing his carpet when they are gone. I have bought for him an aluminium box with his initials on the lid and half a dozen aluminium ashtrays. Three-fourths of the box is filled with cheap Virginians and another compartment with good straight-cut and Egyptian. It hasn't cost me much, but it will make him a king on Sundays.

# "An English Opinion of the American Christmas Cards."

FROM *HARPER'S BAZAAR*, DECEMBER 23, 1882

On the occasion of an interesting exhibition of English and American Christmas Cards recently held in London, the leading London ladies' paper, the *Queen*, of October 21st, 1882, says, after dwelling on the merits and demerits of the various products:

"Sorry as we are for the honor of the old country to confess it, but proud as we are for the honor of the young daughter over the sea to acknowledge it, we *do* acknowledge that, for artistic conception and imaginative rendering, added to beauty of execution, the cards of Messrs Prang, of Boston, distance every other."

After describing several of Prang's cards, it says further: "but beyond all, for depth of meaning and power, is a card bearing the motto 'Good Tidings of Great Joy'—a homeless mother with her children, standing under a leafless, snowladen tree, have a glorious vision of the Virgin Mother with the Babe in her arms. This is a true 'Christmas Card.'"

The card referred to above is after the design of Miss Dora

Wheeler, which gained in Prang's last exhibition the first artist's prize of one thousand dollars, and the first popular prize of one thousand dollars; and Miss Wheeler may well be proud of that third additional prize of honor, coming from a source generally chary of its praise for American art.

Prang's American Christmas Cards are for sale in every art store.—[Adv.]

135

# "What to Give on Christmas Day"

FROM *THE LADIES' HOME JOURNAL*, DECEMBER 1902

Lists of Possible Presents for Journal Readers to Give.

Each recurring Christmas Day finds the world more in love with the idea of giving and of scattering gifts broadcast so that none may be forgotten. To help all those who need any advice as to what they should give in the way of Christmas presents to those in their own homes, as well as to those outside of their immediate circle, the following lists have been prepared.

## FOR THE GRANDMOTHER OF THE FAMILY

| | | |
|---|---|---|
| *Lace Fichu* | *Lace Collar* | *Vinaigrette* |
| *Lorgnette* | *Easy chair* | *Footstool* |
| *Side Combs* | *Bureau Silver* | *Traveling Bag* |
| *Workbag* | *Gold Thimble* | *Gold Pen* |
| *Screen* | *Rocking chair* | *Silk Shoulder* |
| *Shawl* | *Afghan* | *Clock with White* |
| *Face* | *Fan* | *Writing Tablet* |
| *Portfolio* | *Eiderdown Jacket* | *Sofa Pillow* |
| *Hemstitched Collar and Cuffs* | | |

## For the Grandfather

| | | |
|---|---|---|
| Silver Key Chain | Tally Pencil | Morris Chair |
| Reading Lamp | Pair of Slippers | Housecoat |
| Cane | Umbrella | Sofa Pillow |
| Warm Gloves | Pulse Warmers | Paper Cutter |
| Book Marker | Desk Calendar | Magnifying Glass |
| Letter File | A Bright and Warm Afghan | |

## For the Mother

| | | |
|---|---|---|
| Growing Plant | Flowers | Pretty Fan |
| Vinaigrette | Sofa Pillow | Afghan |
| Breakfast Jacket | Flannel Kimono | Handmade Nightdresses |
| Slippers | Lace Veil | Gloves |
| Lace Tie | Collars and Cuffs | Piece of Bureau Silver |
| A Calendar | Veil Pin | Bonnet Pin |
| Shell Hairpins | Lace Fichu | Feather Boa |
| Hemstitched Handkerchiefs | | Traveling Writing Tablet |

Let the different members of the family surprise her by having some new photographs of themselves taken, and give them to her in a pretty leather case. And if she needs a new traveling bag, or an umbrella, or a card case, or a chatelaine bag, supply her need in as generous a way as possible.

## For the Father

| | | |
|---|---|---|
| Fob | Something for his Desk | Scarfpin |
| Wallet | Dress-Suit Protector | Silver Key Ring |

| | | |
|---|---|---|
| Cigar Jar | Ashtray or Pipe | Shaving-Paper Case |
| Shaving Mirror | Military Hairbrushes | Clothesbrush |
| Good Almanac | Calendar | Paper Cutter |
| Reading Lamp | Homemade Bathrobe | |

If you want to please him very much, give him a new photograph of your mother in a pretty leather frame. If he needs a new umbrella, cane, or traveling satchel, give him one or the other.

## For the Elder Sister

| | | |
|---|---|---|
| Desk | Bookshelf | Picture |
| Chair | Some Photographs | Clock |
| Burnt-Wood Outfit | Chafing Dish | Candlestick |
| Chatelaine | Card Case | Bureau Silver |
| Gold or Silver Thimble | Workbag | Muff Chain |
| Muff | Japanese Kimono | Silk Petticoat |
| Monogram Stationery | Seal | Lace Collar |
| Fan | Bonbonnière | Vinaigrette |
| Belt Buckle | Belt Pin | Gloves |
| Glove Box | Chiffon Boa | Point d'Esprit Fichu |
| Short Gold Neck-Chain | Hatpin | Indian Necklace |
| Bracelet | Locket or Pendant | Gold Barrette |
| Long Chain | Trinkets | Shoe Buckles |
| Slippers | Pretty Rose Bowl | |

Where money needs to be considered, an odd chair or table, a comfortable lounge, a good rug, a cheval glass, or a piece of old-fashioned mahogany furniture would delight the heart of any girl, and make her Christmas a very joyful one indeed.

## FOR THE YOUNG MAN IN THE FAMILY

| | | |
|---|---|---|
| *Sleeve Buttons* | *Studs* | *Watch Chain* |
| *Fob* | *Photographs* | *Desk* |
| *Dressing Case* | *Bureau Silver* | *Traveling Bag* |
| *Wallet* | *Cigar Case* | *Cigarette Case* |
| *Dress-Suit Case* | *Gloves* | *Card Case* |
| *Penknife* | *Gold Pencil* | *Paper Cutter* |
| *Scarf Pin* | *Seal Ring* | *Stamp Case* |
| *Key Ring* | *Golf Stockings* | *Golf Vest* |
| *Opera Glass* | *Field-Glass* | *Matchbox* |
| *Cigar Cutter* | *Camera* | *Camera Folio* |
| *Cane* | *Leather Collar-Box* | *Golf Clubs* |
| *Golf Bag* | *Fancy Coat Hanger* | *Satchel Tag* |
| *Sofa Cushion* | *Linen Table Cover* | |

*A Good Picture for His Room*

## WHAT TO GIVE A LITTLE GIRL

For the little daughter of the house there is a long list, which includes:

| Dolls | Doll's Furniture | Games |
| Paper Dolls | Workbox | Workbag |
| Chair | Table | Bureau Silver |
| Jewel Box | Desk | Bookshelf |
| Skates | Tennis Racket | Set of Furs |
| Party Dress | Shoe Buckles | Party Slippers |
| Monogram Paper | Desk Fittings | Ring |
| Neck-Chain | String of Beads | Chatelaine Watch |
| Chatelaine Bag | Music Roll | Kate Greenaway Toilet Set |
| Chair | Red Waterproof Coat and Red Umbrella | |

*Photographs of her father and mother may be added to this list.*

## For the Twelve-Year-Old Boy

| Football | Football Suit | Baseball |
| Catcher's Glove | Games | Box of Paints |
| Watch | Chain | Studs |
| Sleeve Buttons | Microscope | Desk |
| Indian Clubs | Bicycle | Face Mask |
| Bicycle Clock | Pedometer | Lantern |
| Dumbbells | Skates | Rubber Boots |
| Sweater | Boxing Gloves | Punching Bag |
| Penknife | Toolbox | Printing Press |
| Some Type | Typewriter | Clock |
| Stamp Book | Stamps | A Good Map of the World |

## For the Six-Year-Old Boy

| | | |
|---|---|---|
| Train of Cars | Blocks | Locomotive |
| Track | Skates | Sled |
| Football | Sweater | Sleeve Buttons |
| Collar Button | Paintbox | Tool Chest |
| Transparent Slate | Tin Soldiers | Boat |
| Express Wagon | Hoop and Stick | Humming Top |
| Soldier Suit | Small Tent | A Dog |
| Some Rabbits | Start a Bank Account for Him | |

## What to Give the Baby

| | | |
|---|---|---|
| Dress Studs | Bib Pin | Mother Goose |
| Spoon | Silver Rattle | Carriage Pillow |
| Lace Bib | Carriage Boots | Afghan |
| Rag Doll | Punchinello | Flannel Kimono |
| Knitted Blanket | Woolly Dog | Woolly Sheep |
| A Baby's Journal | | |

## Presents for the Minister

| | | |
|---|---|---|
| Reading Lamp | Easy Chair | Wallet |
| Cardcase | Fountain Pen | Book Rack |
| Silver Key Ring | Sermon Case | Stamp Case |
| Traveling Bag | Subscriptions to Magazines | Portfolio |
| A Good Calendar for 1903 | | |

## For the Invalid

Who is for the time being shut away from outside pleasures the following list will answer:

| | | |
|---|---|---|
| Flowers | Fruit | Easy Chair |
| Low Table | Night Lamp | Hand Mirror |
| Folding Screen | Pretty Tray | Woolen Afghan |
| Sofa Pillow | Silk Jacket | Bed Slippers |
| Crystal Vase | Cracker Jar | Thermometer |
| Night Clock | Piece of China, Glass or Silver | |

## For the Servants of the Family

For the members of your household who have served you faithfully during the year, and who you hope will continue to do so during the coming one, your gifts should take any form save that which is suggestive of work. Money is always welcomed, particularly if it be a piece of gold or a new banknote in a pretty purse. Other gifts are:

| | | |
|---|---|---|
| Stationery | Writing Tablet | Waterproof Coat |
| Umbrella | Marked Handkerchiefs | Gloves |
| Belt | Necktie | Underclothes |
| Collars and Cuffs | Clock | Neck Ribbon |
| Work Basket Well-Fitted | | |

A nice present for a nursemaid, when it can be afforded, is a substantial trunk or traveling bag.

In the household where many servants are kept, a Christmas present which will please them all will be a brand new piece of furniture, a new rug, or a new carpet for their sitting room.

## The People on the Immediate Outside

When Christmas comes, the members of establishments and households, where it is possible, should endeavor to remember all with whom they have come in contact during the year preceding this most blessed day in the year.

The postman, the policeman on duty in your vicinity, the newsboy, the woman who comes in occasionally for a day's work, the seamstress, and the teacher of your child can all be remembered. But whatever you give, give in an unostentatious a manner as possible, remembering the Bible injunction: "Let not thy left hand know what thy right hand doeth."

# "Victorian Dolls"

FROM *HARPER'S BAZAAR*, DECEMBER 31, 1881

"The eating doll is the novelty with which girls are delighted this year. A bit of candy is put in her open mouth, disappears, and comes out at the sole of her foot. Another new doll has music within herself, so that when wound she raises her hands and seems to sing. A third novelty, more valued for its durability than beauty, has the doll head cut from a solid piece of wood, and this wooden head can he banged about without breaking. The head moves, and the body, which is also of wood, is painted as the fine French dolls are; and some of these wooden dolls say "Mamma" and "Papa." In small sizes, such dolls, without the speaking attachment, are $1.25, and these are chosen for children whose bump of destructiveness is large. The well-known indestructible heads, with short hair of sheep's wool that will wash and comb, are made with prettier faces than when first introduced."

"Brown-eyed dolls are in great favor this season, especially among the bisque dolls, that were formerly all blue-eyed. The tiny doll, entirely of bisque, with natural long blonde hair, eyes that open and close, and jointed limbs, is a favorite with little girls who do not think size everything; and these cost from sixty-five cents upward."

"Mothers who want to teach their children correct ideas select each part of the doll with care, and have each article of clothing well made, so that it can be taken off and put on. First, the doll's head is selected. This may be of the composition said to be indestructible, and with short blonde curly hair of wool that is easily cleansed, and will cost from thirty cents to two dollars, according to size; or else it may be of French bisque, with eyes that are fixed or with movable eyes, and hair of wool, but most natural-looking. These range from seventy cents upward, and among the more expensive heads are those with Titian red hair and brown eyes, or else golden yellow hair with a bang on the forehead and flowing behind. The wax heads are most varied of all and most natural-looking, but most perishable. They are shown as infants with bald heads or a scant bang, to wear caps; as short-haired boys, with Charles II flowing locks; and as ladies with elaborate coiffures."

"The body is then chosen of either muslin or kid, and must be made up without wires, and stuffed with cotton to make it light, instead of the heavy sawdust that sifts through the cover. They can also be bought with the crying arrangement inside. The muslin bodies cost from thirty cents upward; those of kid are more expensive."

"Mother Hubbard dolls are favorites this season, and as this consists in dressing them in a shirred cloak of cashmere or satin, with a poke bonnet or steeple-crowned hat of the same, they are easily gotten up at home. The imported dolls come elaborately arrayed in plush and satin costumes, but tasteful little girls prefer instead a doll dressed in the first short clothes with white muslin yoke dresses, skirts, and petticoats that may be taken off and put on, and over this a Mother Hubbard hard cloak, with hat to match. Every article of clothing may be bought separately for the doll, including rubber overshoes and hairpins, and there are boxes with three or four different sets of clothing for the doll inmate."

When circumstances do not permit of a tree, an easy way to make little children happy is to heap all their Christmas gifts in front of an empty fireplace so as to give them the appearance of having been hastily dumped down the chimney. On top of all, place a note of apology from Santa Claus, setting forth that he was so busy that he found it really impossible to leave his sleigh and come down into the house with the presents. The novelty of it all will be likely to delight the children.

FROM *THE LADIES' HOME JOURNAL*, DECEMBER 1903

PLUM

PUDDING

IS A TRULY NATIONAL DISH, AND

REFUSESTO FLOURISH OUTSIDE OF

ENGLAND. IT CAN OBTAIN NO

FOOTING IN FRANCE. A FRENCHMAN

WILL DRESS LIKE AN ENGLISHMAN, SWEAR LIKE

AN ENGLISHMAN, AND GET DRUNK LIKE

AN ENGLISHMAN; BUT IF YOU WOULD OFFEND

HIM FOREVER, COMPEL HIM

TO EAT PLUM PUDDING.

—Thomas K. Harvey, The Book of Christmas,
Boston: Robers Brothers, 1888

# Christmas Food

# "Fine English Plum Pudding"

FROM *THE LADIES' HOME JOURNAL*, DECEMBER 1904

## Mrs. S. T. Rorer

Stone a pound of raisins; mix with them one pound of currants, half a pound of minced, candied orange peel, three-quarters of a pound of breadcrumbs, one pound of suet that has been shredded and chopped fine, a quarter of a pound of flour, a quarter of a pound of brown sugar, half a nutmeg grated and the grated rind of one lemon. Beat five eggs without separating the whites from the yolks, and add half a pint of good grape juice; mix this with the dry ingredients, working the whole thoroughly until the mixture is moist but not wet.

Pack in greased moulds, or small tin kettles; cover, and steam or boil continuously for ten hours. Take the puddings from the water, remove the lids and cool in the moulds. Next morning the lids may be replaced and the puddings put aside for two, three or four weeks, until needed. The longer they stand the better. But do not overlook the important point that they should be kept in a cool place.

> plum pudding is a truly national dish, and refuses to flourish outside of england. it can obtain no footing in france. A frenchman will dress like an englishman, swear like an englishman, and get drunk like an englishman; but if you would offend him forever, compel him to eat plum pudding.
> —Thomas K. Hervey, *The Book of Christmas*. Boston: Roberts Brothers, 1888

# "Christmas Breakfast, Luncheon and Tea"

FROM *THE LADIES' HOME JOURNAL*, DECEMBER 1902

## Mrs. S. T. Rorer

The first meal on Christmas Day should be well balanced and consist of the lightest and most easily digestible foods. This of all meals should be carefully looked after, as it starts the day. Eggs are to be the first selected as they are satisfying and easy of digestion; serve them either soft-boiled, steamed or made into omelets.

To my way of thinking the perfect Christmas breakfast is composed of daintily baked apples served hot with whipped cream, brown bread and butter, followed, if you like, by a cup of French coffee. Broiled sweetbreads, tripe or mutton chops are light and if taken in small quantities will not overtax the digestive organs.

The Christmas dinner is full and quite satisfying and frequently composed of food which is slow of digestion. For this reason let the tea or luncheon be of light and easily digested foods. If luncheon is served at noon and dinner at night great care must be taken not to satisfy the appetite and spoil the full enjoyment of the Christmas dinner. If dinner is served at about two o'clock serve the tea as an informal collation late in the evening. If, however, dinner is to be served at six o'clock it will be necessary to have a light luncheon at twelve o'clock or not later than twelve-thirty. Select appetizing foods for the Christmas luncheon. For instance, sardines, chipped beef, sandwiches, oysters, brown bread and butter, beef a la mode with cold tomato sauce, and a small cup of clear coffee or tea. Do not serve fruits or sweets. Candies, which are usually standing close at hand on that day, are frequently nibbled at; these will take the place of dessert and will allow a sharper appetite for the dinner. As a first course sardines may be served cold with a garnish of parsley and lemon, or they may be broiled and dished on toast: or oysters simply panned. Bouillon is appetizing, not satisfying, and is frequently passed alone with a wafer to take the place of a fuller luncheon. Cold dishes are not always acceptable in cold weather, but they are frequently more satisfying than some of the lighter hot ones.

When dinner is served at noon the tea should be exceedingly light and composed of such dishes as chicken and nut sandwiches, a cup of weak tea, zwieback and hot milk. Clam bouillon and wafer, followed by creamed sweetbreads cooked in the chafing dish are always acceptable.

# A Few Menus for Christmas

## BREAKFASTS

Oatmeal; Milk; Poached Eggs, Toast; Coffee
Baked Apples, Cream; Broiled Sweetbreads; Gems; Coffee
Stewed Prunes; Oatmeal, Cream; Toast; Coffee

## LUNCHEONS

Bouillon in Cups; Omelet with Peas, Celery; Rolls,
Cheese; Coffee
Deviled Oysters, Toasted Brown Bread; Tomato Jelly,
Wafers; Baked Apples with Cream
Oyster Bouillon; Broiled Chops, Peas, Celery with French
Dressing; Lemon Jelly, Whipped Cream

## TEAS

Chicken in Aspic, Mayonnaise Dressing; Olives,
Salted Almonds, Celery
Oyster Salad, French Dressing; Brown and White Bread
Sandwiches; Olives, Salted Almonds; Coffee
Chicken and Nut Sandwiches; Tea;
Lemon Jelly in Sponge Cups
Fruit Sandwiches; Cocoa; Olives, Salted Almonds,
Bonbons

*from*

# Some Christmas Menus

FROM *THE LADIES' HOME JOURNAL*, DECEMBER 1903

Mrs. S. T. Rorer

## Christmas Dinners

Tomato Soup, Croutons

Roast Chicken

Oyster or Giblet Sauce

Cranberry Jelly

Browned Mashed Potatoes

Creamed Onions

Cabbage Salad, Wafers

Brown Betty With Raisins

Cider Sauce

Coffee

Homemade Peanut Brittle and Chocolates

### (FROM 1904)

Sardine Canapes

Oysters on Half Shell

Salted Almonds

Olives

Consommé

Creamed Fish
and Chili Sauce

Small Rolls

Roasted Turkey
and Giblet Sauce

Cranberry Jelly

Sweet Potato Croquettes

Creamed Onions

Scalloped Oysters

Broiled Birds

Celery With French
Dressing

English Plum Pudding
and Hard Sauce

Coffee

Turkish Soup, Croutons

Celery

Olives

Roasted Ribs of Beef

Brown Sauce

Cole Slaw

Plum Pudding

Hard Sauce

Coffee

Candies

Nuts

Brown Stock Soup

Croutons

Roasted Capon, Oyster Sauce,
Cranberry Jelly

Sweet and White Potatoes

Stewed Celery

Apple and Cabbage Salad
in Apple Cases

Wafers, Nefchatel Cheese

Huntsman Pudding,
Orange Sauce

Coffee

Bonbons, Salted Almonds

## VEGETARIAN DINNER

Mock Oyster Soup,
Crackers

Rice Timbale with
Mushrooms

Mock Turkey (Nuts and
Hominy), Tomato Sauce

Cranberry Jelly

Boiled Onions

Apple and Chicory Salad

Wafers

Plum Pudding
(without suet)

Jelly Sauce

Salted Nuts

Bonbons

Coffee

# A FISH DINNER

Oysters on Half Shell,
  Crackers

Cream of Spinach Soup

Boiled Cod, Sauce
  Hollandaise

Potato Balls, Scalloped
  Tomatoes

A Plain Gateau

Horseradish, Tabasco
  Sauce, Lemon

Crackers

Cheese

Nuts

Candies

Fruits

# "When a Light Christmas Dessert is Wanted"

FROM *THE LADIES' HOME JOURNAL*, DECEMBER 1900

## Mrs. S. T. Rorer

Such sweets as plain charlottes are perhaps the least deadly of all desserts. Cream is a very valuable fatty food, and when it is whipped it is light and far better to follow a heavy meat dinner than puddings, which are rich in egg and mile. To whip well, cream must be at least thirty-six hours old, of good quality and very cold. Put it into your "whipper," if you have one, turn rapidly for a moment and it will be one mass of air bubbles. Turn this into a basin, stand in another of cracked ice. For one pint of cream allow half an ounce of gelatine, two-thirds of a cupful of powdered sugar and one teaspoonful of vanilla. Cover the gelatine with a quarter of a cupful of cold water, soak while you whip the cream, then stand it over the teakettle to melt. Sprinkle the sugar over the cream, add vanilla and at last the gelatine. Stir at once and continuously until well mixed and slightly thickened. Turn into a fancy mould or plain one lined with sponge cake or lady-fingers. Two hours in a cold place will set it, or it may stand in a very cold place over night.

# "Kitchens of the Rich"

FROM *THE BROOKLYN DAILY EAGLE*, DECEMBER 22, 1889

PREPARING CHRISTMAS DINNERS IN FIFTH AVENUE
CORNELIUS VANDERBILT'S COOK CAN PROVIDE FOR
A THOUSAND GUESTS—JAY GOULD HAS AN
OLD-FASHIONED CHICKEN PIE ON THANKSGIVING DAY

Columns have been written about the uptown parlors and boudoirs, but not a word about that most important of all rooms, the kitchen. When the guests assemble for Christmas dinner, reportorial pens will be busy giving detailed accounts of the dining rooms, the dinner service, the decorations and all that; they will even reproduce the daintily decorated menu cards, but the real thing—the food—without which the most gorgeous feast would be a flat failure, is left alone. How to prepare a seventeen-course dinner for five hundred guests and have everything, down to the minutiae of a bit of linen or a silver fork, exactly as it should be, requires some thought and training and more appliances than one would dream of. The most spacious private kitchen in New York is that of Cornelius Vanderbilt, at 1 West Fifty-Seventh street. It is forty feet long by twenty wide. The floor is laid in small squares of brown and white marble, the walls are of pressed brick and the whole of one side and end is filled with closets. Through the glass doors one can see upon the shelves every sort of utensil which the most exacting housekeeper could desire. This kitchen is beautifully lighted, as it is in the front part of the basement, on a level with the street and has two very large stained glass windows. The chef is a pleasant young German who is evidently very proud of his position.

"You have a very large range," remarked the writer. "The largest I have ever seen in a private family."

"Yes," replied the chef, "but sometimes I must prepare for a thousand people."

"And you do it alone?"

"Why, certainly: that is, I do all the cooking. You know I have nothing to with preparing the food: there are ten servants who attend to that."

"Do you have anything extra for Christmas?" was the next query.

"Why, no: we could not have," was the reply. "We get the best there is in the market every day. The only difference will be the number of people to provide for."

I had noticed that all the cooking dishes are of copper and I asked why this was so.

"Because," said the chief, as he lifted the cover from a huge baking dish, "copper is cleaner than anything else and it holds the heat better. You cannot brown meat in anything as you can in copper. Now, this is for a roast. You see this cover fits closely. I prepare the roast—say it is a turkey or a little pig—and I put it inside this dish and shut it up tight. I do not open it again until it is done. I only turn the dish over once in ten minutes."

"But how can you tell when it is done?"

"Very easily. In the first place I have my oven at exactly the right heat. You see here is an indicator that tells me just how hot it is," pointing to a tube just inside the oven door. "Then I weigh the roast and allow just fifteen minutes to a pound. At that time it comes out crisp and brown, done to a turn, with all the flavor and juices retained. Not even the steam can escape. That is the only way to roast a Christmas turkey."

I don't think Mrs. Vanderbilt visits her kitchen very often. But when she does she will find the great copper range with its six broad fireplaces and great copper roof, sinks, tables, floors and all, as clean as can be. Even the blonde chef's white linen suit is as spotless as snow.

Mr. Frederick Vanderbilt lives at 459 Fifth Avenue, in the old Vanderbilt home. It was here that William II lived before he removed to the mansion on Fifty-second street, from which he was buried. The kitchen is an old-fashioned one, is below the street and is dark and damp. Gas is burning all day long. The servants when at dinner sit at two long tables in the kitchen.

There is no chef here. His place is occupied by a Frenchwoman, who has the girth of a typical cook. She explained in her broken English that, though the family had nothing different for dinner on Christmas Day, the servants had. And she took me unto the servants' parlor, which was not only comfortable but in some respects elegant.

The floor was covered with dark blue felt, over which a large rug was laid. Sofas, easy chairs, pictures and pretty curtains gave a very cozy and homelike air to the place. Some old ornaments of rosewood and gilt were scattered about, and in the center of the room stood a large table. Upon this the Christmas gifts for the servants are placed, and they are always of value. A special order is given for the servants' dinner. On this day each one of the help is allowed a pint of good old burgundy, and at some time during the day each is allowed to go out for an hour or two. Mrs. Fred Vanderbilt is one of the Ladies Bountiful to the poor. A Christmas feast, most of which is prepared in her own kitchen, is served at her mission, and a present for each child is provided by herself. The hours which most society women spend in bed are devoted by Mrs. Vanderbilt to her various beneficiaries, one of whom remarked, "St. Peter ought to swing the gates open wide when she comes in."

At 8 East Thirty-third street is the home of William Waldorf Astor, who believes in the good old English custom of filling Christmas Day with good Christmas cheer. The chef, a broad-faced Frenchman, seemed to thoroughly enjoy the prospect of the good things he was going to prepare, particularly the plum pudding. Everybody in the land will surely be interested to know what the ingredients of this pudding are. Here is the receipt:

Suet, two pounds: raisins, two pounds; citron, one pound; English plums, two pounds; molasses, one pint; twelve eggs; cloves, cinnamon, mace and nutmeg, each one ounce; one teaspoon salt; one tablespoon soda; one pint best brandy; flour for a stiff batter. Tie the mixture in a well-greased pudding cloth and steam four hours. Serve with brandy sauce, hot and plentiful.

Mrs. Astor's kitchen is comparatively small, but there is a separate dining room for the servants, so the chef has it all to himself. He had finished a plateful of delicate chocolate eclairs for lunch and was just beginning on a salad. I noticed that here the cooking dishes were of porcelain and spoke of it.

"Mr. Vanderbilt's chef can have all the copper dishes he wants," said the Frenchman, sententiously. "I'll take the porcelain every time; it's easier to keep clean and I'm sure it is more wholesome, and as for roasting" (with a self-satisfied smile), "I'll place my roast beef beside his on Christmas Day, if he likes, and anyone may choose."

The Astor kitchen has a hardwood floor, polished to the smoothness of glass. Everything is kept out in the scullery until ready for the oven, so there is no refuse.

The home of Mr. A. M. Palmer at 25 East Sixty-fifth street, has the most beautifully light and clean kitchen imaginable, and in it is a cook who makes you think of the old days when in Mother's kitchen at home you reveled in doughnut horses and gingerbread men. Her very presence suggests a good dinner.

"Have you dined at A. M. Palmer's" asked Charles Wyndham the other day of a brother actor. "Then you have not known the full delight of living."

"What are you going to have for Christmas dinner?" I asked the cook.

"I don't know yet, madam," she answered; "Mrs. Palmer has not given her orders; but I suppose it will be something extra, though here we have Christmas every day of the year."

"A. M. Palmer's is a typical New England kitchen, with its oaken floor and shining tins. I looked instinctively for the cat that should have been purring by the fire.

In Jay Gould's methodical home everything is done by clockwork. The servants are given every Monday morning their bills of fare for the week and are expected to carry out the programme without more ado. There is one thing in the Gould household as unchangeable as the Median Law. On Thanksgiving day an old-fashioned chicken pie is prepared just as his mother used to make it. So the great Wall Street speculator has a touch of sentiment in his makeup after all. Miss Helen Gould is the housekeeper and is as methodical as her father. Everything in the domestic economy of that house moves as if on well-oiled hinges.

The palatial home of Henry M. Cook, the great Wall Street banker, corner of Seventy-eighth street and Fifth Avenue, has a kitchen like the interior of a grand salon. The walls and floor are of solid white marble; the tables have marble tops and all the appliances for cooking are of the most expensive sort. It takes a small corps of servants to keep the inside of the kitchen clean.

Mrs. Cleveland's kitchen is a sunny place and is favored with visits from its mistress oftener than most of the others which I have mentioned. The cookery is very simple and is done by a broad-shouldered Scotchwoman.

"We will hae turkey and Christmas pudding on Christmas Day," she said. "But nae company; th'master does na like company on holidays."

The range and tinware in the kitchen shone like French mirrors. She had no need to fear visitors at any time.

The dining room has the quaint admonition carved over the great oaken fireplace:

> Some hae meat an'canna eat
> An' some wad eat that want it;
> But we hae meat an' we can eat,
> An' sae: "Let the Lord be thankit."

# "One Christmas Feast"

FROM THE *NEW YORK DAILY TRIBUNE*, DECEMBER 12, 1901

## How a Woman Entertains Fifty Guests for Twenty Dollars

Giving a dinner to fifty poor children in one's home sounds like a big undertaking. Few householders indeed have ever considered the feasibility of feeding such a large number of waifs at one time, and fewer still understand that a dinner of this sort is one of the easiest and least expensive ways of doing good in allopathic doses.

There is one society woman, though, in New York who has found it out. In her opinion, dinner giving of this particular variety is superior to any other known variety of banquet in the pleasure it gives all round, and in its far-reaching results.

"Feeding them is the least important feature of the entertainment," she said yesterday. "You cannot imagine how my small guests appreciate being entertained in a private house instead of a hired hall, and I know that in their case the effect of an environment of refinement, together with courteous attention even for so short a time, is wonderfully lasting. Children are impressionable little beings."

"Where do you get your guests?" asked a listener.

"I go to one of the large East Side missions and ask for fifty little girls (so far I haven't had the courage to take boys) to come to me at noon a day or two before Christmas or the day after, whichever suits me best, and I do the same things at Thanksgiving and again in Easter week. My guests are different each time.

"A mission worker accompanies the children to my house and takes them back again to the quarter in which they live. They come in at the front door and the leave their wraps at the rear end of the hall before going down to the front basement where the dinner is spread on two long tables reaching from end to end of the room.

"After they have eaten their fill the children come trooping upstairs into my dining room at the rear of the drawing room where I greet them and chat with them a while before opening the folding doors, on the other side of which at Christmastime is a big tree dressed with lighted candles and trinkets and containing a little present for each child.

"The delight of the little girls and their efforts to be as polite as their surroundings warrant are charming to see, and give me more pleasure than anything else connected with the Christmas holidays. At Thanksgiving I give them a Punch-and-Judy show for an afterpiece, and at Easter I distribute candy eggs and other trifles.

"The cost of the entertainment aside from the presents is small—not more than twenty dollars unless the menu includes turkey. I found out, however, that very poor children have a wonderful respect and liking for beefsteak: that is more of a novelty to them than turkey. They often choose it, in fact, when given a preference, therefore I make beefsteak the pièce de résistance of these dinners.

"Here is an itemized bill of my last dinner, which speaks for itself."

The bill reads thus:

| | |
|---|---|
| *Oysters, eight quarts* | *$3.00* |
| *Milk, ten quarts* | *.50* |
| *Beefsteak, fifteen pounds* | *$2.10* |
| *Corn, twelve cans* | *$1.20* |
| *Sweet potatoes, one hundred* | *$1.00* |
| *Soda crackers, seven pounds* | *.42* |
| *Bread, four loaves* | *.20* |
| *Butter, four pounds* | *$1.00* |
| *Ice cream, six quarts* | *$2.10* |
| *Cakes, one hundred* | *$3.00* |
| *Car fares* | *$5.25* |
| ***Total*** | **$19.77** |

"I always ask a few of my own friends in to see the children," concluded the speaker, "and by that means I have induced some of them to follow my example."

# "Christmas Food Prices"

FROM *THE WASHINGTON POST*, DECEMBER 23, 1915

The abundance of game and the unusual quality of turkeys are the only evidences of winter in the Washington markets. Fresh fruits and vegetables are as plentiful as in springtime, and prices are far less than expected by even the most hopeful. Sales have been brisk, and dealers are unanimous in stating the Christmas marketing was never more satisfactory.

## SEA FOOD

Terrapins, each 50c. to $3.50.

Perch, a pound, 18c.

Large baking fish, a pound, 25c.

Rockfish, a pound, 20c.

Shrimps, a pound, 30c.

Sea trout, a pound, 20c.

Scallops, a quart, 50c.

Brook trout, a pound, 50c.

## GAME

Wild ducks, each, $1.50.

Squabs, each, 35c. to 50c.

Mallards, each, $1.25.

Rabbits, each, 35c.

Redhead ducks, each, $1.50.

Wild geese, a pound, 40c.

Ruddies, each, 60c. to 75c.

Possums, each, 50c. to $1.50.

Quail, each, 50c. to 60c.

# DAIRY PRODUCTS

Philadelphia unsalted butter, a pound, 65c.

Best print butter, 45c. to 50c.

Best tub butter, a pound, 45c.

New York cream cheese, a pound, 25c.

Gorgonzola cheese, a pound, 50c.

Liederkranz, a package, 15c.

Snappy cheese, a cake, 10c.

Domestic sweitzer, a pound, 35c.

Sapsago, a cake, 10c.

A new Swiss cream cheese, a box, 50c.

Brie, a cake, 25c.

Roquefort, a pound, 50c.

Camembert, a cake, 35c.

Parmesan, a pound, 50c.

Elgin, each, $1.50.

# POULTRY

Turkeys, a pound, 28c. to 30c.

Fowls, a pound, 22c.

Baking chickens, a pound, 23c.

Fryers, a pound, 30c.

Broilers, a pound, 35c.

Guinea hens, a pound, 28c.

Domestic ducks, a pound, 30c.

# BEEF

Prime rib roasts, a pound, 25c.

Short rib roasts, a pound, 20c.

Chuck roasts, a pound, 18c.

Round steak, a pound, 25c. to 30c.

Sirloin steak, a pound, 30c.

Tenderloin steak, a pound, 35c.

Filet of beef, a pound, $1.

Soup bones and soup meat, a pound, 15c. to 18c.

# LAMB

Legs of lamb, a pound, 25c.

Breasts of lamb, a pound, 18c. to 20c.

Shoulder chops, a pound, 25c.

French chops, a pound, 35c.

Lamb's liver, a pound, 30c.

# VEAL

Veal cutlets, a pound, 35c.

Veal chops, a pound, 30c.

Breasts of veal, a pound, 25c. to 30c.

Veal liver, a pound, 45c.

Calves' heads, each, 35c. to 50c.

Sweetbreads, $1 to $1.25 a set.

# PORK

Fresh hams, a pound, 20c.

Cured Virginia hams, a pound, 22c.

Spare ribs, a pound, 15c.

Fresh shoulders, a pound, 15c.

Pork sausage, a pound, 25c.

Sliced bacon, a pound, 24c. and 30c.

Sliced ham, a pound, 25c. to 28c.

Pigs' feet, a set, 40c.

Heads, each, 30c. to 50c.

# FRUITS

Hothouse grapes, a pound, $1.

Cassava melons, each, 35c. to 75c.

California grapes, a pound, 15c. to 20c.

Japanese persimmons, a dozen, 75c.

Torelle pears, a dozen, 95c.

Winter Nells pears, a dozen, 60c.

Malaga grapes, a pound, 25c. to 30c.

Qumquats, a quart, 20c.

Lady apples, a quart, 25c.

Pineapples, each, 20c. to 25c.

Tangerines, a dozen, 40c.

Grapefruit, each, 8c. to 15c.

Oranges, a dozen, 25c. to 60c.

Table apples, a dozen, 50c. to 60c.

## VEGETABLES

French artichokes, each 20c.

Dasheens, a pound, 15c.

Lima beans, in shell, a peck, $1.75.

French endives, a pound, 60c.

Brussels sprouts, a quart, 20c.

New potatoes, a quart, 10c.

Celery roots, each, 15c.

Bullnose peppers, a dozen, 80c.

Squash, each, 20c.

Pumpkins, each, 20c. to 25c.

Cabbage, a head, 8c. to 10c.

Red cabbage, a head, 20c. and 25c.

Oysterplant, a bunch, 8c.

Carrots, a bunch, 10c.

Eggplants, each, 15c. and 20c.

Green peas, in shell, a peck, $1.50

# "Christmas Cakes"

From *The New York Daily Tribune*, December 23, 1900

In German households Christmas cake-making is a part of the festive ceremonials, and the good housewives would as quickly think of turning Santa Claus from their doors as of turning over their holiday baking to a hireling. Among the good things that they make at this season are Berliner *Pfannkuchen*—in plain English, raised doughnuts with jelly filling. The time occupied in their making is fully recompensed by the results.

Put into a bowl four cupfuls of sifted flour, a quarter teaspoonful of salt, and one tablespoonful of sugar. Make a hollow in the centre of the mixture and pour into it one yeast cake that has been dissolved in half a cupful of tepid milk. Melt one-fourth cupful of solid butter. Add it to one cupful of warm milk and turn into the bowl. If the milk and butter are hot they will kill the yeast. Add the yolks of eight eggs and mix the whole into a soft dough. Cover the bowl with a cloth and set in a warm place until the dough has risen to double its original height. Then take half the dough, put it on a floured moulding board that is not cold, and roll it into a sheet about a quarter of an inch thick; cut it into rounds with a cake cutter. Brush these with beaten egg and place in the center of half the number a teaspoonful of marmalade or of fruit jelly. Cover these with the remaining half of the rounds, press the edges together and cut out again with a cutter which is a little smaller than the first one.

Put them on a floured napkin in a warm place and cover with a napkin. They should rise to double their height in half an hour. Meanwhile repeat the process with the other part of the dough. Fry in deep hot fat, the same as crullers, keeping them turning constantly while they are in the kettle. When done, remove to blotting paper and roll in powdered sugar. The "Berliners" are considered best while hot, but many people serve them for breakfast with coffee.

Among the favorite small cakes are peppernuts. Cream together one-half pound of lard, one cupful of solid butter and two cupfuls of brown sugar. Add to this three eggs, beating them in one at a time and stirring thoroughly after each is added. To this add one grated nutmeg, two teaspoonfuls of cinnamon, one teaspoonful of ground clove, two teaspoonfuls of ground aniseed, two ounces of whole coriander seeds, one-half pound of chopped almonds and one-fourth pound of chopped citron. Then put in six cupfuls of molasses, with which has been mixed two teaspoonfuls of baking soda dissolved in a little boiling water, and flour with which four teaspoonfuls of cream or tartar has been sifted. Flour sufficient to make a stiff dough should be used. Work the dough with the hands until it is perfectly smooth and the ingredients are thoroughly mixed. Shape it into long rolls about an inch in diameter, and cut these into slices one-fourth of an inch thick. Bake in a quick oven until a light brown, and when cold turn into a cake box, where they will keep an indefinite time.

For almond cookies, blanch one-half pound of sweet almonds and five bitter almonds, and mortar them to a paste with the white of an egg. Cream together one cupful of sugar and one tablespoon of butter. Mix this with the grated rind of one lemon, a salt-spoonful of salt, two cupfuls of flour, two eggs and the almond paste. Work the mixture into a stiff dough. Roll it into a thin sheet, and cut with fancy-shaped cookie cutters. Bake on buttered tins in a medium hot oven.

Biscuit *kippel* are more delicate, and are delicious with ice creams and sherbets. Beat together to a cream one-half cupful of powdered sugar and the yolks of four eggs. Add one cupful of sifted flour and the stiffly beaten whites of four eggs. Drop by teaspoonfuls into paper-lined tins, sprinkle them with sugar and finely chopped almonds, and bake in a slow oven.

In all the above rules, as in all the recipes given in the Household Department of *The Tribune*, a spoonful means a rounded spoonful—that is, not heaped, but rounded over in the same proportion as the spoon is concave.

A cupful of dry material should be heaped lightly (not shaken down), and then, with a knife, leveled across the top, making an even cupful.

When butter is to be melted it is always so stated.

# "Luxurious Economy for Holiday Week"

From *The Ladies' Home Journal*, December 1900

### Mrs. S. T. Rorer

Articles bearing upon economy at the Christmas season are hardly likely to be popular, but there surely is no good reason for extravagance at any time. I should like to convince all women who read the *Journal* that economy should be practiced at all seasons, and particularly at the one where even a little of it may serve to enable the mistress of a home to be more generous than she had expected to be able to be. Turkeys in many parts of the country are expensive at Christmastime. Chicken, when treated turkey fashion, will answer the same purpose. Select a chicken of good size, about a year old. Draw, and hang it in a very cold place three days before roasting. At cooking time stuff it with nicely seasoned mashed boiled chestnuts, and rub the breast with onion. Put into the bottom of the baking pan a slice of bacon and half a cupful of water; place the chicken in the pan in a hot oven, basting every ten minutes until it is brown. Then cool down the oven, and cook at a lower temperature fifteen minutes to each pound. Garnish with parsley or celery tops when sending to the table.

# Here Is a Cheap Christmas Plum Cake

Fruitcake is considered a luxury even at the holiday season, but it is only so when made according to modern methods. With a little thick sour cream, a delicious spice cake, which few people can tell from the best of fruitcake, may be made. Dissolve a level teaspoonful of soda in two tablespoonfuls of warm water; add to it half a pint of very thick sour cream; stir it for a moment; turn it into a bowl, and add half a cupful of New Orleans molasses; mix thoroughly; add half a pint of brown sugar, a tablespoonful of cinnamon, and three and a half cupfuls of sifted pastry flour. The batter must be very thick. Then stir in one pound of raisins that have been stoned and cut into halves and floured. Turn this into a square pan lined with greased paper, and bake in a very moderate oven for an hour and a half, or steam for one hour and bake for the remaining half hour. A cake made with this recipe will keep for a long time—indeed, it grows better with age. It may be iced and decorated as the more expensive cakes are.

# A Substitute for Plum Pudding

Plum pudding, the traditional Christmas pudding, is expensive, and few people can afford either the time to make it or the cost of the materials. Substitute a Saratoga pudding, and few will know the difference. To make one, roll and sift one pint of stale bread crumbs; add one cupful of four, a teaspoonful of cinnamon, half of a grated nutmeg, a cupful of brown sugar, a

pound of seedless raisins, a quarter of a pound of shredded citron, floured, and half a pound of raw suet, freed from mem-
brane and chopped fine; mix thoroughly. Dissolve one
teaspoonful of baking soda in two tablespoonfuls of water, and
add it to one cupful of New Orleans molasses; add one egg well
beaten, the juice and grated rind of one lemon, and pour it into
the dry ingredients. Work all carefully together until it is moist,
not wet, and pack it down into a greased kettle or mould. Cover
and boil continuously for four hours. Lift the lid of the mould
until the pudding is cold, then cover and stand aside. Reheat at
serving time. An ordinary lard kettle may be used in place of a
mould. This pudding may be made a week before Christmas
and heated for the Christmas dinner. Serve hot with hard
sauce.

When one cannot afford a hard sauce the next best thing is
jelly sauce. Put half a tumblerful of currant jelly into a saucepan, and add a pint of water and the juice of one lemon. Moisten
one tablespoonful of cornstarch with a little cold water; add it to
the jelly and water; cook, and stir until thick and smooth. Serve
hot.

## Making All Sorts of Cream Candies

For cream chocolates put a quarter of a pound of fondant into
the smallest of your saucepans; add two ounces of chocolate
melted over hot water; add a teaspoonful of vanilla and a teaspoonful of water. Stand the saucepan in another containing a

little hot water, and stir with the handle of your wooden paddle until the mixture is creamy. If too thick when very hot add a few drops of water until it is proper consistency. Take it to the table, hot water and all; drop in, one at a time, the centers; lift with the dipper, and turn carefully on oiled paper.

After you have finished the chocolates dip the other centres in the same way, using different flavoring. For coffee creams use extract of coffee. For orange, the yellow grated rind of an orange and a little orange juice as it is melting down. For pistachio creams use the chopped nuts, both in centers and coverings, coloring both a light green with a little bruised parsley or spinach.

For creamed dates split the dates and remove the seeds. Roll fondant the same size, put it into the dates, press together, and roll in granulated sugar; or the spaces from which the seeds were taken may be filled with quarters of English walnuts. Split candied cherries, and put in a piece of fondant the size of a cherry stone; press together, and roll in granulated sugar. Put all these on greased papers in a dry place until the next day.

To make creamed English walnuts, roll a piece of fondant the size of an almond; put it on one half of the walnut and press it down with another half, and with the index finger of your right hand pack it into the little crevices, giving it a finished look.

Put bits of nuts left over and some pine nuts into a square greased baking pan. Melt a pound of sugar in a dry saucepan over the fire, stirring constantly. When straw-colored pour it over the nuts and stand them aside.

# One of the Daintiest Christmas Cakes

Ribbon cake is one of the daintiest of Christmas cakes. To make it, beat to a cream half a cupful (a quarter of a pound) of butter; add gradually two cupfuls of granulated sugar, the yolks of four eggs; beat thoroughly; add a teaspoonful of vanilla and one cupful of milk. Beat the whites of four eggs to a stiff froth. Add two teaspoonfuls of baking powder to three cupfuls of pastry flour, and sift; add alternately milk and flour, and stir in the well-beaten whites at the last moment, being careful to mix thoroughly. Take out one-third of the mixture, and add to it a tablespoonful of cinnamon, an ounce of chocolate, melted, a cupful of washed floured currants and a quarter of a cupful (about two ounces) finely shredded citron. Grease three sheet-pans of the same size; put the fruit mixture into one, the other mixture into two pans. Bake in a moderately quick oven for half an hour.

When done, turn the cakes out on oiled paper, spread one light cake with a layer of soft icing, which you have made while the cakes are baking; place the darker cake on top, spread it with icing, and on top of this place the remaining light cake. Cover with a piece of oiled paper, on top of which place one of the pans in which they were baked. At each end place a pound weight; stand aside until cold, then remove the weights. Ice the top with sugar icing, and when "set" cut the whole into diamonds, rounds or squares.

# "Even Those Who Are Forced to Travel on December 25 Need Not Miss the Annual Feast"

FROM *THE NEW YORK DAILY TRIBUNE*, DECEMBER 22, 1901

Going home for Christmas was a task in the early days of the republic, when "home" was many miles away, and even in the "the forties" a winter trip was not an unalloyed pleasure. Foot warmers in the shape of heated stoves and warming pans, with fuel supply, had to be taken, in addition to the regular supply of blankets and robes, and no outfit was complete without hampers and baskets with food to last during the trip. In the office of one of the great transportation companies there hangs a picture which shows the difficulties connected with a Christmas journey in the time usually referred to as "before the war."

The sleigh in which the young couple, with baby, Christmas boxes and baskets, are making the trip from town to the old homestead is shown almost hopelessly stalled in a snowdrift. A glimpse of rescuers a long distance away is the only thing that gives one hope that the party may possibly reach its destination.

The incident of the picture was an extreme case, but even without a snowstorm, with "good going," there were hardships connected with these pleasure trips which the present generation in this part of the country knows little about. The roadside tavern and the hospitable farmhouse could always be counted upon when the horse fell lame, when the food gave out, or when shelter was necessary, but on the long stretches between these hospitable roofs there was often much discomfort, and it took much time to reach the place of destination.

"They were good times, and no one ever has so much fun nowadays as we had then," said a venerable champion of the good old days of long ago, "and going home for Christmas, or going visiting in those days was more fun, no matter how little comfort we had, than you can have now with all your modern arrangements." When the picture of the snowed-under family party was shown to him he said: "That's nothing. They liked it, and were none the worse for it. They didn't think the baby would die the next day it if got good and cold, and women didn't get nervous fits in those days just because they got stuck in a snowdrift. I'll bet that little family party ate more when they reached Grandma's for one meal than their descendants now eat in three, and they enjoyed what they ate too, and didn't have to consult their doctor's 'don't list' every time they took a bite."

The good old days are always the brightest, and everybody admired the old man for his enthusiasm, but the young man of today is perfectly willing to hear about the snow-coaches of his grandfather's time; and, taking it for granted that they were charming means of conveyance, that an atmosphere of romance surrounded them, and that the old-time journey consumed less nerve tissue, he prefers the methods of today and wishes they were even more rapid. Going home for Christmas from New York by the modern means of travel is a pleasure which those people enjoy the most who have known the defects of early railroad travel. The trains make rapid time, they are elaborately furnished and equipped, and those people who cannot reach their destination in time for Christmas dinner need not be deprived of that luxury, for a Christmas dinner while one travels at the rate of fifty or sixty miles an hour is one of the possibilities of the present system of transportation. The dining car, although it is one of the newer features of the American railway system, has become an absolute necessity, and because of its popularity the various railroad companies now find it necessary to have an annex which is conducted like departments of a modern hotel. Great quantities of food supplies must be handled and stored: table linen, silver-, glass-, and chinaware must be carried, and a force of men employed to handle, store, and cook for and serve patrons of the road at stations and in the cars.

The New York Central Railroad operates twenty-one dining cars between New York, Buffalo and Boston, and manages the restaurants at Weehawken, Kingston, Poughkeepsie, Albany, Troy, Utica, Syracuse, Rochester and Buffalo. At the restaurants the supplies are usually bought in the home markets, but the cars receive their stocks through New York, which is the purchasing center.

About thirty to forty persons can dine in a car at one time, but the supplies are usually sufficient to feed several "sets" and it is nothing unusual to have a dining car filled three times on a run between New York and Albany. "And all we serve," said J. T. McKee, the superintendent of the service, "is prepared in our own kitchen on the train." One often hears people say that the dining car dinner comes out of a tin can. As a matter of fact, there has never been a morsel of canned meat bought by us and we never even use canned vegetables when we can get the fresh article."

One of the latest features in the system is the day coach with a kitchen attachment. Seven of these cars are in operation on the New York Central road, and George H. Daniels, the general passenger agent of the road, says that they have been a source of much comfort to passengers, who, until they traveled in one of these coaches, never knew that one could be served with a meal on a train anywhere except in the regular dining car. The New York Central serves, in its various dining places, about eight thousand meals a day and the menu on the dining cars is so choice that no special Christmas menu will be arranged. "But it will be a good Christmas dinner, nevertheless," said one of the dining car servicemen, "and will be as good as most hotel dinners on that day."

On the Pennsylvania system dining cars are stocked in Jersey City for Pittsburgh, Washington, Philadelphia and Buffalo. Of the twenty cars in the service, nine are stored with supplies every day. The menu is agreed upon, and then knowing the usual number of people patronizing the train, the stock is put on board and prepared. The company has many relay stations at which supplies may be taken on in case of shortage, and these sources are frequently drawn upon, because the object is to have everything fresh. The company has restaurants at Baltimore, Pittsburgh, Washington, and Philadelphia, in addition to the fine establishment at Jersey City, which is looked upon as perfect in all its appointments.

The Central Railroad of New Jersey also has dining car service on board its beautifully-equipped fast trains, and people who travel by that route need not miss their Christmas dinner.

# Old Santy Claus

# "On Santa Claus"

FROM *CHRISTMAS: ITS ORIGIN, CELEBRATION AND SIGNIFICANCE AS RELATED IN PROSE AND VERSE.* EDITED BY ROBERT HAVEN SCHAUFFLER. NEW YORK: MOFFAT, YARD AND CO., 1913.

George A. Baker, Jr.

Brave old times those were. In the first half of the seventeenth century, we mean; before there was any such place as New York and Manhattan Island was occupied mostly by woods, and had a funny little Dutch town, known as New Amsterdam, sprouting out of the southern end of it. Those were the days of solid comfort, or mighty pipes, and unctuous doughnuts. Winter had not yet been so much affected by artificiality as he is nowadays, and was contented to be what he is, not trying to pass himself off for Spring; and Christmas—well, it was Christmas. Do you know why? Because in those times Santa Claus used to live in a great old house in the midst of an evergreen forest, just back of the Hudson, and about halfway between New Amsterdam and Albany. A house built out of funny little Dutch bricks, with gables whose sides looked like staircases, and a roof of red tiles with more weathercocks and chimneys sticking out of it than you could count. Phew, how cold it was there! The wind roared and shouted around the house, and the snow fell steadily half the year, so that the summers never melted it away till winter came again. And Santa Claus thought that was the greatest pleasure in life: for he loved to have enormous fires in the great fireplaces, and the colder it was, the bigger fires he would have, and the louder the winds roared around his chimney. There he sat and worked away all the year round, making dolls, and soldiers, and Noah's arks, and witches, and every other sort of toy you can think of. When Christmas Eve came he'd harness up his reindeer, Dasher, and Prancer, and Vixen, and the rest of them, and wrap himself up in furs, and light his big pipe, and cram his sled full of the doll-babies and Noah's arks, and all the other toys he'd been making, and off he'd go with a great shout and tremendous ringing of sleigh bells. Before morning he'd be up and down every chimney in New Amsterdam, filling the stout grey yarn stockings with toys, and apples, and gingerbread, laughing and chuckling so, all the while, that the laughs and chuckles didn't get out of the air for a week afterwards.

But the old house has gone to ruin, and Santa Claus doesn't live there any longer. You see, he married about forty years ago; his wife was a Grundy, daughter of old Mrs. Grundy, of Fifth Avenue, of whom you've all heard. She married him for his money and couldn't put up with his plain way of living and his careless jollity. He is such an easy-going, good-natured old soul, that she manages him without any trouble. So the first thing she did was to make him change his name to St. Nicholas; then she made him give up his old house, and move into town; then she sent away the reindeer, for she didn't know what Ma would say to such an outlandish turnout; then she threw away his pipe because it was vulgar, and the first Christmas Eve that he went off and stayed out all night she had hysterics, and declared she'd go home to her Ma, and get a divorce if he ever did such a thing again. She'd have put a stop to his giving away toys every year, too, only she thought it looked well, and as it was, she wouldn't let him make them himself any more, but compelled him to spend enormous sums in bringing them from Paris, and Vienna, and Nuremberg.

So now Santa Claus is St. Nicholas, and lives in a brownstone house on Fifth Avenue, a great deal handsomer than he can afford, and keeps a carriage, not because he wants it, but because Mrs. Shoddy, next door, keeps one; and loves, not to be jolly himself and to make everybody else so, but to please his wife's mother. He has to give an awful pull, what with his wife's extravagance, and the high prices of Parisian and Viennese toys, to make both ends meet, although he does speculate in stocks, and is very lucky. Instead of looking forward to Christmas with pleasure, and thinking what a good time he will have, he pulls out his ledger, and groans, and wonders how on earth he's going to make his presents this year, and thinks he would stop giving them entirely, only he's so mortally afraid of his mother-in-law, and he knows what she'd say if he did. So he borrows money wherever he can, and sends over to Paris for fans, and opera glasses, and bonbon boxes, and jewelry and when they come he sits down in his parlor and lets his wife tell him just what to do with them. So she takes out her list and runs over the names; she had all the rich people down, for she is a religious woman, and the Bible says "unto him that hath, it shall be given." This is the way she talks: "The little Croesuses could help you very much in business. And there are the Centlivres; we must pick out something magnificent for them; they give a party Christmas night: of course the presents will be on exhibition, and I shall sink with shame if anyone else's are handsomer than ours." So she goes on, until all the rich people are disposed of. Then Santa Claus asks: "How about the Brinkers, my dear?" The Brinkers are great favorites of his. "Good gracious, dearest! How often have I told you, you mustn't manifest such an interest in those Brinkers? What would Ma say if she knew you associated with such common people!" "But I'm Dutch myself, pet." "Of course you are, darling, but there's no need of letting every one know it!" St. Nicholas hardly dares to do it, but he finally suggests very meekly: "The poor children, my darling." "Bother the poor children, my dear!" They're a most affectionate couple, you know. Then St. Nicholas sighs and sighs, and sends for his messengers, and they all come in with long faces, and take off big packages to the Croesuses and the Centlivres, and the rest of them. The messengers do their work entirely as a matter of business, so there isn't a sign of a laugh, nor a symptom of a chuckle in the air the next day. The little Croesuses first cry, because they haven't received more, and then fight over what they have; they then eat too much French candy, and get sick and cross, and the whole house is filled with their noise. So Mamma has a headache; and Papa longs for his office, and misses the tick-tick of the stock telegraph, and thinks what a confounded nuisance holidays are. That is what Christmas is like in good society.

But I must tell you a secret. Away up in the fourth story of his grand house, where his wife never goes, St. Nicholas has a little workshop, and there he sits whenever he gets a chance, making the most wonderful dolls, and gorgeous soldiers, and miraculous jumping jacks, and tin horns—such quantities of tin horns! Someone ought to speak to him about those tin horns. But after all, they please the poor children, so we suppose it's all right. Now do you know what he does with these things? On Christmas Eve he gets his old sled down from the stable away up by the North Pole, and as soon as his wife is fast asleep, he puts on his old furs and gets out from under his shirts in his bureau drawer a Dutch pipe, three times as big as the one his wife threw away, and off he goes. He tumbles down all the poor people's chimneys, and fills up the stockings to overflowing, and plants gorgeous Christmas trees in all the mission schools.

He has a glorious good time, and laughs and chuckles tremendously, except when, once in a while, he thinks of what would happen if his wife found him out.

So there's a little fun going on after all.

Do you know, if it were not for this performance of his, we should wish with all our heart that St. Nicholas were dead and buried. But we must say, we wish his wife would die, and that all the Grundy family would follow her good example, for between them they've spoiled a good many jolly people besides St. Nicholas.

# "Santa Claus's Farewell"

FROM NEW YORK DAILY TRIBUNE, DECEMBER 23, 1900

## M.D.F.

Another Century has passed. I think my Time has Come

To say Goodby to ancient ties, and hie to my last Home.

I've led a busy Life, 'tis true, and yet I'm loath to Go.

But the Rising Generation have no use for me, I know.

Ah, Children! whose Ancestors I knew and Loved as You.

The Saint your Fathers reverenced Must make his last Adieu.

For Centuries my name has been a Household one, I trow.

But Times and Customs are so Changed, You do not Need me
  now.

My Fortress at the far North Pole will soon be reached by Men,

My Sleigh and Reindeers out of place with Trolley Cars, and then

Electric Carriages exist, to take the Place of all.

And Santa Claus without his Team won't be a Saint at all.

The Chimneys that I clambered down Have long been leveled
  low.

With other Innovations, these also Had to go.

The simple Offerings that I brought were Tokens of the Love

That Christ the Master showed for us in Coming from Above

But now the thought is Give and Take, and That was not my
  Plan.
When as the Chosen Patron Saint I came from Amsterdam
To New York, then Nieuw Amsterdam, Fort Orange, and the
  Rest,
Who, peopled by a Holland Race by a Dutch Saint were blest.
I asked them Nothing in return, Save that the Young New Year
Be welcomed with a Open house, full of Good Will and Cheer.
Alas, that too is out of Date, and so with Aching heart,
I say Goodby, the modern Ways and I are quite Apart.
God grant the Century, near at hand, may teach the Coming Race
To Reverence the Fathers' ways. Honor the Fathers' place,
And in the Bustle of that Life, Oh! Bid your Children pause
To Treasure some Fond Memory of poor Old Santa Claus.

# "An Old-Fashioned Christmas Party"

FROM *THE LADIES' HOME JOURNAL*, DECEMBER 1903

Mrs. Julia H. Richer

These invitations, written on sheets of white notepaper, at the top of which were painted sprays of holly, were received by a number of children a week before Christmas.

> Mrs. And Mrs. James Ross
> Invite you to spend
> Christmas Eve
> With their daughter
> Violet
> Santa Claus will call
> For you at 6:00 p.m.
> 304 Main Street

Promptly at six o'clock on the day appointed a sleigh drawn by two horses with their harness strung with sleigh bells, and old Santa Claus resplendent in a suit of red and brown, and looking decidedly jolly, called, as arranged, for each invited guest, and while driving home from house to house entertained them with tales of the "North Pole," his workshop and his reindeer. The merry party drove to the residence of the hostess and found it decorated with holly and mistletoe. Each child was first asked to guess the number of berries on a large piece of mistletoe which hung from one of the chandeliers. The one guessing nearest the correct number received a stickpin bearing a tiny enameled spray of mistletoe.

Then came romping old-fashioned games, after which a Christmas carol was sung and the children marched in to supper. A star-shaped table had been arranged for the occasion. In its center was a rather small but handsomely decorated tree. The refreshments consisted of turkey sandwiches, cocoa, lemon jelly with whipped cream, sponge cake, bonbons and nuts. The sponge cake was baked in small star-shaped pans, and ornamented with red-and-white icing.

When supper was over Santa Claus took from the tree a number of small stockings and gave one to each child. Each one contained bonbons and a small gift.

After two Christmas recitations by a "grown-up," Santa Claus bade his host and hostess "Good night," and the merry children drove off with him.

# "Christmas Merrymaking"

FROM *THE NEW YORK DAILY TRIBUNE*, DECEMBER 23, 1900

## End-of-the-Century Innovations in Festivities—High Prices Paid for Drawing Room Entertainments.

How to entertain the children, of smaller and larger growth as well—for all are children on Christmas Day—is one of the problems of the season. The giving of expensive entertainments in private homes is an end-of-the-century innovation in this country. Thirty years ago these were limited to music, lectures, and recitation, with sometimes the help of a humorist. Since that time there has been a growing tendency to copy England in employing professionals, and now talent is engaged for private houses at a cost ranging from fifteen dollars for Punch and Judy to two thousand dollars for opera stars. Five years ago a vaudeville entertainment for a private house or club would not have been considered high class. Today it is the fad, and has been elevated almost to the standard of the musical field. For the little ones Punch and Judy is as fascinating as it was to their forebears, and Santa Claus in velvet robe and cap, his long white beard still bristling with the icy winds of the snow country, is just as captivating as ever.

"Mamma," shrieked a youngster last year, as the good saint, bearing his load, pranced into the room. "ask him to stay to supper!"—this being the acme of hospitality according to baby ideas.

"You can ask him," responded the mother; and Alfred, seizing Santa Claus by the coat gave a pressing invitation.

"To supper," exclaimed a particle of perturbation, turning to his mother and said, "Why, Mamma, he looks just as if he ate a lot."

As Santa Claus was Uncle Jack, whose appetite has never been known to fail him, this unplanned part of the program received hearty applause.

Another little boy had determined to satisfy his curiosity as to Santa Claus's mode of entrance to the house, and escaping from his mother's vigilance discovered the saint eating bonbons in the butler's pantry. Rushing back to the assembled family in the library, he shouted: "Santa Claus has come! He got down somehow and is eating candy in there!"

This year this youngster, remembering Santa Claus's sweet tooth, insisted on leaving a box of candy marked "For Santa Claus" in his stocking. Strange as it may seem, when the stocking was explored in the morning the candy was gone and in place of it was a note of thanks signed "Santa Claus."

The marionettes, so popular among the French children, who support with their pennies traveling shows of the kind in the Champs Élysées and other Paris parks, is liked equally well by young America, and has become one of the favorite among parlor entertainments. It consists of a stage, with settings, scenes, properties and costumed figures, the latter about three feet in height. The entertainment includes a ballet, a prima donna, who comes in and with the aid of a ventriloquist renders popular songs; a balloon ascension, a mechanical Turk, etc. The dancing skeleton, perhaps more than all, delights the youngsters. For while he dances his bones suddenly fall apart and lies scattered on the floor. Then, before there is time to recover from the amazement at the calamity they begin to gather themselves together until again the perfect skeleton whirls about the stage.

Magic always delights the younger members of the family, and the man who takes an empty handkerchief and produces a live rabbit or bird, or who throws a handful of coins into the crowd is regarded as more than mortal. The old fashioned humorist and the palmist, too, always entertain, but nothing perhaps brings wilder cheers than the animal man, who, appearing in the skins of various domestic and wild animals, imitates their cries and antics. The shadowgraph is another never-failing source of amusement. An entire play, the actors of which are the ten fingers and thumbs of a deft pair of hands, is a part of the program for one home. A house will appear on the sheet, and beneath the window serenaders. A pail of water thrown from the window submerges the singers and a policeman appears upon the scene and takes them off. Cinderella and other fairy and nursery tales in brilliantly-colored moving pictures are among the newest pleasure-giving schemes.

Merry revel will be heard in many country houses which have

been kept open until after the holidays, and to supply these, as well as city homes, with suitable entertainment will tax to the utmost the entertainment bureaus.

While the children's entertainment will in most cases occupy the morning or afternoon of Christmas Day, that for the grownups will be given in the evening. For these, vaudeville performances are more popular, and cost the most. These, of course, necessitate large rooms and a stage. Other and simpler modes of amusement are found in musical programs for which soloists, quartets, minstrels, bands, orchestras, etc., can be procured. Comedians, storytellers, caricaturists and monologists help to make an enjoyable evening.

*from*

# "The Young Mother's Calendar"

FROM *THE LADIES' HOME JOURNAL*, DECEMBER 1904

Emelyn Lincoln Coolidge, M.D.,
of the Babies' Hospital, New York City

## What to Do on Christmas

As Christmas seems to belong to the children more than to any one else, we naturally want to make this season an especially happy one for them; but now, as at all times, the wise mother will remember how peculiarly delicate are the nervous systems of her children, and exercise a little common-sense judgment in planning their holiday pleasures.

Let the children believe in the dear old Santa Claus as long as possible; they should be allowed to hang up their stockings on Christmas Eve and wake up Christmas morning to find them well filled; but when they are capering about the room at bedtime or before being dressed in the early morning the mother should see that they are well protected from the cold by means of warm little wrappers made of eiderdown cloth or else blanket wrappers. On their feet let them wear little bedroom slippers made of either knit or crocheted wool.

The stockings might contain a bright red apple and an orange, a few simple toys and a box of gumdrops, peppermints or some animals made of barley sugar and wrapped in numerous layers of paper, as it will be more fun to undo the bundles and at last come upon the hidden treasures. Some of the fruit may be eaten for breakfast, and after breakfast a little of the candy.

## What Not to Do on Christmas

*Don't allow the child to eat rich poultry, as goose, duck and turkey, or rich desserts, as pies, plum pudding, anything fried, or nuts and raisins.*

*Don't allow him to eat chocolate of any kind or highly colored candy*

*Don't allow him to eat between regular meals*

*Don't allow him to sit up late*

*Don't take him to the theater unless he is at least ten years old, and then only to children's matinees once or twice a year*

*Don't allow him to attend parties if he is at all inclined to be nervous*

*Don't give him elaborate presents, such as mechanical toys*

*Don't allow him to have a great quantity of presents all at once*

*Don't spend a large sum of money in trying to make him happy when a smaller amount would answer a great deal better*

*Don't allow him to give up his regular outdoor exercise because he would rather play in the house with his new toys*

*Don't allow him to be selfish and forget those less fortunate than himself*

*Don't allow him to be destructive*

*Don't allow him to leave his toys for someone else to pick up*

*Don't allow him to read new books for several hours at a time until he ruins his eyes and makes his head ache*

*Don't forget that a dose of castor oil and a common-sense mother will often save a large doctor's bill*

*from*

# "Inexhaustibility of the Subject of Christmas"

FROM *CHRISTMAS: ITS ORIGIN, CELEBRATION AND SIGNIFICANCE AS RELATED IN PROSE AND VERSE*. EDITED BY ROBERT HAVEN SCHAUFFLER. NEW YORK: MOFFAT, YARD AND CO., 1913.

## Leigh Hunt

Observe a little boy at a Christmas dinner, and his grandfather opposite him. What a world of secret similarity there is between them! How hope in one, and retrospection in the other, and appetite in both, meet over the same ground of pudding, and understand it to a nicety! How the senior batters the little boy on his third slice! And how the little boy thinks within himself that he dines that day as well as the senior! How both look hot and red and smiling, and juvenile. How the little boy is conscious of the Christmas box in his pocket! (of which, indeed, the grandfather jocosely puts him in mind); and how the grandfather is quite as conscious of the plum, or part of a plum, or whatever fraction it may be, in his own! How he incites the little boy to love money and good dinners all his life! And how determined the little boy is to abide by his advice—with a secret addition in favor of holidays and marbles, to which there is an analogy, in the senior's mind, on the side of trips to Hastings, and a game of whist! Finally, the old gentleman sees his own face in the pretty smooth one of the child; and if the child is not best pleased at his proclamation of the likeness (in truth, is horrified at it, and thinks it a sort of madness), yet nice observers, who have lived long enough to see the wonderful changes in people's faces from youth to age, probably discern the thing well enough, and feel a movement of pathos at their hearts in considering the world of trouble and emotion that is the causer of the changes. *That* old man's face was once like that little boy's! That little boy's will be one day like that old man's! What a thought to make us all love and respect one another, if not for our fine qualities, at least for the trouble and sorrow which we all go through!

Ay, and joy too; for all people have their joys as well as troubles, at one time or another, most likely both together, or in constant alternation. And the greater part of troubles are not the worst things in the world, but only graver forms of the requisite motion of the universe, or workings towards a better condition of things, the greater or less violent according as we give them violence, or respect them like awful but not ill-meaning gods, and entertain them with a rewarded patience. Grave thoughts, you will say, for Christmas. But no season has a greater right to grave thoughts, in passing; and, for that very reason, no season has a greater right to let them pass, and recur to more light ones.

So a noble and merry season to you, my masters; and may we meet, thick and threefold, many a time and oft, in blithe yet most thoughtful pages! Fail not to call to mind, in the course of the 25<sup>th</sup> of this month, that the divinest Heart that ever walked the earth was born on that day; and then smile and enjoy yourselves for the rest of it; for mirth is also of Heaven's making, and wondrous was the wine-drinking at Galilee.

# "Is There a Santa Claus?"

FROM *THE LADIES' HOME JOURNAL*, DECEMBER 1903

## By Jacob A. Riis

"Dear Mr. Riis:

"A little chap of six on the Western frontier writes to us:

"'Will you please tell me if there is a Santa Claus? Papa says not.'

"Won't you answer him?"

That was the message that came to me last December just as I was going on a journey. Why the editor of *The Ladies' Home Journal* sent it to me I don't know. Perhaps it was because, when I was a little chap, my home was way up toward that white north where even the little boys ride in sleds behind reindeer, because they are the only horses they have. Perhaps it was because when I was a young lad I knew Hans Christian Andersen, who surely ought to know, and spoke his tongue. Perhaps it was both. I will ask the editor when I see him. Meanwhile, here was his letter, with Christmas right at the door, and, as I said, I was going on a journey.

I buttoned it up in my greatcoat along with a lot of others I didn't have time to read, and I thought as I went to the depot what a pity it was that my little friend's papa should have forgotten about Santa Claus. We big people do forget the strangest way, and then we haven't got a bit of a good time anymore.

No Santa Claus! If you had asked that car full of people I would have liked to hear the answers they would have given you. No Santa Claus! Why, there was scarce a man in the lot who didn't carry a bundle that looked as if it had just tumbled out of his sleigh. I felt of one slyly, and it was a boy's sled—a "Flexible Flyer," I know, because he left one at our house the Christmas before—and I distinctly heard the rattling of a pair of skates in that box in the next seat. They were all good-natured, everyone, though the train was behind time—that is a sure sign of Christmas. The brakeman wore a piece of mistletoe in his cap and a broad grin on his face and he said, "Merry Christmas" in a way to make a man feel good all the rest of the day. No Santa Claus, is there? You just ask him!

And then the train rolled into the city under the big gray dome to which George Washington gave his name, and by-and-by I went through a doorway which all American boys would rather see than go to school a whole week, though they love their teacher dearly. It is true that last winter my own little lad told the kind man whose house it is that he would rather ride up and down in the elevator at the hotel, but that was because he was so very little at the time and didn't know things rightly, and besides, it was his first experience with an elevator.

As I was saying, I went through the door into a beautiful white hall with lofty pillars, between which there were regular banks of holly with the red berries shining through, just as if it were out in the woods! And from behind one of them there came the merriest laugh you could ever think of. Do you think, now, it was that letter in my pocket that gave that guilty little throb against my heart when I heard it, or what could it have been? I hadn't even time to ask myself the question, for there stood my host all framed in holly, and with the heartiest handclasp.

"Come in" he said, and drew me after. "The coffee is waiting," and he beamed upon the table with the veriest Christmas face as he poured it out himself, one cup for his dear wife and one for me. The children—ah! you should have asked *them* if there was a Santa Claus!

And so we sat and talked and I told my kind friends that my own dear old mother, whom I have not seen for years was very, very sick in faraway Denmark and longing for her boy, and a mist came into my hostess' gentle eyes and she said, "Let us cable over and tell her how much we think of her," though she had never seen her, and it was not sooner said than done. In came a man with a writing pad, and while we drank our coffee this message sped under the great stormy sea to the faraway country, where the day was shading into evening already though the sun was scarce two hours high in Washington:

The White House
*Mrs. Riis, Ribe, Denmark*:
Your son is breakfasting with us. We send you our love and sympathy.

*Theodore and Edith Roosevelt*

For, you see, the house with the holly in the hall was the White House, and my host was the President of the United States. I have to tell it to you, or you might easily fall into the same error I came near falling into. I had to pinch myself to make sure the President was not Santa Claus himself. I felt that he had in that moment given me the very greatest Christmas gift a man ever received: my little mother's life. For really what ails her is that she is very old, and I know that when she got the President's dispatch she must have become immediately ten years younger and got right out of bed. Don't you know mothers are that way when anyone makes much of their boys? I think Santa Claus must have brought them all in the beginning—the mothers I mean.

I would just give anything to see what happened in that old town that is full of blessed memories to me when the telegraph ticked off that message. I will warrant the town hurried out, burgomaster, bishop and all, to do honor to my gentle old mother. No Santa Claus, eh? What was that, then, that spanned two oceans with a breath of love and cheer, I should like to know. Tell me that!

After the coffee we sat together in the President's office for a little while while he signed commissions, each and every one of which was just Santa Claus's gift to a grown-up boy who had been good in the year that was going; and before we parted the President had lifted with so many strokes of his pen clouds of sorrow and want that weighed heavily on homes I knew of, to which Santa Claus had had hard work finding his way that Christmas.

It seemed to me as I went out the door, where the big policeman touched his hat and wished me a Merry Christmas, that the sun never shone so brightly in May as it did then. I quite expected to see the crocuses and the jonquils that make the White House garden so pretty out in full bloom. They were not, I suppose, only because they are official flowers and have a proper respect for the calendar that runs Congress and the Executive Department, too.

I stopped on the way down the avenue at Uncle Sam's paymaster's to see what he thought of it. And there he was, busy as could be, making ready for the coming of Santa Claus. No need of my asking any questions here. Men stood in line with banknotes in their hands asking for gold—new gold pieces, they said, most every one. The paymaster, who had a sprig of Christmas green fixed in his desk just like any other man, laughed and shook his head and said, "Santa Claus?" and the men in the line laughed too and nodded and went away with their gold.

One man who went out just ahead of me I saw stoop over a poor woman on the corner and thrust something into her hand, then walk hastily away. It was I who caught the light in the woman's eye and the blessing upon her poor wan lips, and the grass seemed greener in the Treasury dooryard, and the sky bluer than it had been before, even on that bright day. Perhaps—well, never mind! If anyone says anything to you about principles and giving alms you tell him that Santa Claus takes care of the principles at Christmas, and not to be afraid. As for him, if you want to know, just ask the old woman on the Treasury corner.

And so, walking down that Avenue of Good-Will, I came to my train again and went home. And when I had time to think it all over I remembered the letters in my pocket which I had not opened. I took them out and read them, and among them were two sent to me in trust for Santa Claus himself which I had to lay away with the editor's message until I got the dew rubbed off my spectacles. One was from a great banker, and it contained a check for a thousand dollars to help buy a home for some poor children of the East Side tenements in New York, where the chimneys are so small and mean that scarce even a letter will go up through them, so that ever so many little ones over there never get on Santa Claus's book at all.

215

The other letter was from a lonely old widow, almost as old as my dear mother in Denmark, and it contained a two-dollar bill. For years, she wrote, she had saved and saved, hoping some time to have five dollars, and then she would go with me to the homes of the very poor and be Santa Claus herself. "And wherever you decided it was right to leave a trifle, that should be the place where it would be left," read the letter. But now she was so old that she could no longer think of such a trip and so she sent the money she had saved. And I thought of a family in one of those tenements where father and mother are both lying ill, with a boy, who ought to be in school, fighting all alone to keep the wolf from the door, and winning the fight. I guess he has been too busy to send any message up the chimney, if indeed there is one in house; but you ask him, right now, whether he thinks there is a Santa Claus or not!

No Santa Claus? Yes, my little man, there is a Santa Claus, thank God! Your father had just forgotten. The world would indeed be poor without one. It is true that he does not always wear a white beard and drive a reindeer team—not always, you know— but what does it matter? He is Santa Claus with the big, loving, Christmas heart, for all that; Santa Claus with the kind thoughts for everyone that makes children and grown-up people beam with happiness all day long. And shall I tell you a secret which I did not learn at the Post-Office, but it is true all the same—of how you can always be sure your letters go to him straight by the chimney route? It is this: send along with them a friendly thought of the boy you don't like; for Jack who punched you, or Jim who was mean to you. The meaner he was, the harder do you resolve to make it up: not to bear him a grudge. That is the stamp for the letter to Santa. Nobody can stop it, not even a cross-draught in the chimney, when it has that on.

Because—don't you know, Santa Claus is the Spirit of Christmas; and ever and ever so many years ago when the dear little Baby was born after whom we call Christmas and was cradled in a manger out in the stable because there was not room in the inn, that Spirit came into the world to soften the hearts of men and make them love one another. Therefore, that is the mark of the Spirit to this day. Don't let anybody or anything rub it out. Then the rest don't matter. Let them tear Santa's white beard off the Sunday-school festival and growl in his bearskin coat. These are only his disguises. The steps of the real Santa Claus you can trace all through the world as you have done here with me and when you stand in the last of the tracks you will find the blessed Babe of Bethlehem smiling a welcome to you. For you then will be home.

# Acknowledgments

My thanks go to Sheryl Stebbins, Jena Pincott, Laura Neilson, Beth Levy, and Nora Rosansky of Random House Reference. The staff of the New York Public Library was most helpful.

I am very grateful to Arin Lawrence, whose keen editorial eye was instrumental in making this book. Arin was a diligent researcher, a discerning reader and she made sure the book didn't roll completely off the scheduling rails.

# Index of
# Titles and First Lines

221

222